HF
5549.5
.R44
H28
1999

HWBI

Chicago Public Library

R0128437206

Finding & keeping great employees.

BUSINESS/SCIENCE/TECHNOLOGY DIVISION
CHICAGO PUBLIC LIBRARY
400 SOUTH STATE STREET
CHICAGO, IL 60605

D1058562

FINDING &

KEEPING

GREAT

EMPLOYEES

FINDING &
KEEPING
GREAT
EMPLOYEES

JIM HARRIS, PH.D.
JOAN BRANNICK, PH.D.

AMACOM
American Management Association

New York • Atlanta • Boston • Chicago • Kansas City • San Francisco • Washington, D.C.
Brussels • Mexico City • Tokyo • Toronto

This book is available at a special
discount when ordered in bulk quantities.
For information, contact Special Sales Department,
AMACOM, an imprint of AMA Publications, a division of
American Management Association,
1601 Broadway, New York, NY 10019

This publication is designed to provide accurate and authoritative
information in regard to the subject matter covered. It is sold with
the understanding that the publisher is not engaged in rendering
legal, accounting, or other professional service. If legal advice or
other expert assistance is required, the services of a competent
professional person should be sought.

Library of Congress Cataloging-in-Publication Data

Harris, Jim
    Finding & keeping great employees / Jim Harris and Joan Brannick.
        p.   cm.
    Includes bibliographical references and index.
    ISBN 0-8144-0454-5
    1. Employees—Recruiting.   2. Job satisfaction.   3. Labor
turnover.   I. Brannick, Joan.   II. Title.
HF5549.5.R44H28   1999
658.3—dc21   98–41139
                                                                  CIP

© 1999 Jim Harris and Joan Brannick.
All rights reserved.
Printed in the United States of America.

This publication may not be reproduced,
stored in a retrieval system,
or transmitted in whole or in part,
in any form or by any means, electronic,
mechanical, photocopying, recording, or otherwise,
without the prior written permission of AMACOM,
an imprint of AMA Publications, a division of
American Management Association,
1601 Broadway, New York, NY 10019.

Printing number

10   9   8   7   6   5   4   3   2   1

BUSINESS/SCIENCE/TECHNOLOGY DIVISION
CHICAGO PUBLIC LIBRARY
400 SOUTH STATE STREET
CHICAGO, IL 60605

RO 128437206

To my wife, Brenda, and my son, Jason; may God mold me into the husband and father you each deserve.

—Jim

▼ ▼ ▼ ▼ ▼

To my husband, Michael, for your love, support, and patience; I could not have done this without you. To my parents, John and Wanda Posey, for teaching me the values of love, respect, persistence, and hard work; all have served me well.

—Joan

CONTENTS

PREFACE

"Hiring, retaining, and developing great people is the biggest challenge and single greatest key to the success of any business."

—Scott McNealy, CEO, Sun Microsystems

Few business leaders would disagree with McNealy. Many companies, however, consciously or unconsciously create roadblocks that prevent them from accomplishing this important goal. They are unable or unwilling to focus their efforts on a common vision. They create policies and procedures that make it difficult to find and keep the kind of employees they want. They do not allocate the time, money, or additional resources needed to find and keep great employees.

Some companies, on the other hand, truly believe that finding and keeping great employees is their primary challenge, and their actions support the commitment to that challenge. In our opinion, these are the companies we can all learn from. Some of these world-class companies are large, some are small, some of them are well known, and some are unfamiliar to most business leaders. Although different, all of these organizations have one thing in common: They focus on culture. They realize that even though jobs within the company drive *what* is done, their organizational culture drives *how* things are done. Companies with world-class staffing and retention practices see their culture as vital to their organization; they understand culture as the basis for selecting and rewarding people.

The diversity of companies having world-class staffing and retention practices demonstrates that this approach to finding and keeping excellent employees can work in any company. All it takes is strategic commitment to, and committed focus on, the organization's culture. This may not be as easy as it sounds, but the organizational payoffs for such commitment and focus are huge, both financially and nonfinancially.

FROM OUR OWN EXPERIENCE

To be considered an expert in your field, we believe you must have "lived" the topic you are writing about. You must have experienced it not only intellectually but also on a psychological and gut level. It is only through experience that insights and true wisdom emerge.

Our motivation to write this book stems from our own personal experience. We met in 1988 at the headquarters of a Fortune 500 retailer. One of us led the executive and management training function, and the other led the staffing function at a time when the company had 40,000 employees in 1,700 retail operations. Given our responsibilities, we had many opportunities to create and implement programs designed to attract and retain top talent. Although always recognized as top performers, we both left the company. It was not because of job fit, but because of something else. During the last years of our service, we both sensed something was missing. Our careers were progressing, our roles were expanding, and the company was treating us well; but there was a constant, nagging uneasiness within our hearts. After dozens of after-hours skull sessions, and more than our fair share of extended coffee breaks, we finally realized what was missing: a personal sense of feeling deeply connected to the overall purpose of the company.

We also discovered that our previous work experience (in manufacturing, home building, transportation, federal government, and university operations) reflected the cultural connections and disconnections that exist between employer and employees. In some cases, we gave our best; in others, we did not. This was not because of lack of skill, but because we did not feel connected; we didn't feel that our efforts were making a difference.

Many of our professional colleagues and friends have experienced the same disconnection with their employers. Some have resigned to join other companies, and others did so to go into business for themselves. Some of these moves involved more money, but that was not the driving force behind most people's choices. The overwhelming reason these individuals moved from one company to another was that they felt a stronger connection to their new employer's culture. In every case, our colleagues were more dissatisfied with the culture than with their job responsibilities. Beyond these personal experiences, our consulting, speaking, and research have reinforced our belief in the positive power of culture fit. We have seen small, family-owned businesses create a culture that makes people want to work for them and, once there, want to stay. Likewise, we have seen large, publicly traded companies redefine their culture and, through the process, instill commitment to the organization among their employees that is unmatched in their industries.

Some might argue that employees ought to know intuitively how they are connected to the success of the business. Companies should not have to spell it out for their employees. You either get it or you don't, right? Our experience, however, shows us that you cannot count on employees' being able to make the connection on their own. Companies known for their first-rate staffing and retention practices understand that they have a responsibility to create and maintain that connection with their employees. One of the best ways to build such connections is to find employees who support the company's overall core culture, and keep the ones who already do.

The Message of This Book

This book reflects certain fundamental beliefs. First, we believe in people. In our view, people are the real competitive advantage of any company. Having good people decreases turnover, improves individual performance, attracts a flow of new applicants, and fosters growth in organizational profit. We also believe that attracting and retaining the right people is the only way for organizations to succeed in the future.

Second, we believe in corporate culture. Employees can find a job anywhere, but they commit to and want to remain with an organization whose culture they connect with. Certain cultures create and sustain strong cultural connections with their employees. In consequence, these organizations have a significant competitive advantage in finding and keeping great employees. We believe that if there is a strong connection between the core culture and the values of the people, great strides in individual and company performance occur. These organizations understand how critical it is to find and keep people who share the company's core values.

Third, we believe the organizations most successful in their staffing and retention practices are those that leverage their core culture to attract and retain like-valued employees. Although job fit is important, culture fit determines whether someone is highly likely to remain with and be successful with the company. We see job fit as a minimum requirement for companies to be able to find and keep good employees. Focusing on job fit results in hiring someone who can do the job. It does not, however, guarantee that the person wants to do the job or do it well.

Fourth, we believe in a strategic, more than tactical, approach to finding and keeping great employees. In this book, we demonstrate this approach in two ways. First, we outline a strategic framework that fits businesses of any type, industry, or size. We do not present tactical lists (such as ten ways to improve a classified recruitment ad for sales managers). Our approach is to uncover best-practice strategies to help you find and keep excellent employees. We provide examples of how various companies have implemented those best practices. You can then determine how best to apply those strategies to your own company.

Our target audience for this book therefore goes beyond human resources managers to include CEOs, COOs, CIOs, presidents, and operations managers. Further, this book is written for organizations that view the staffing and retention function as a strategic management function, not just a function whose job slots are shoved into the personnel area.

Fifth, we believe in (and have attempted to provide) simple, doable concepts and guidance, rather than rambling, esoteric prose. We believe this book not only provides the strategy and tools to help you focus your organization's efforts but also makes it easier for you to get started in finding and keeping culturally aligned employees of excellence.

Sixth, we believe that any attempt to find and keep great employees must be flexible. Although we describe four basic core cultures, we realize that within those cultures some staffing and retention practices are more effective than others. We do not believe that one size fits all. For our approach to be successful in your company, you need to customize it to your culture.

Finally, we believe that this book can make a significant difference in organizations—a difference in performance, in productivity, and in profitability.

We hope it works for you.

ACKNOWLEDGMENTS

We could name hundreds of people here, but we promise to limit these acknowledgments to those who most directly and profoundly contributed to this manuscript.

Adrienne Hickey, executive editor at AMACOM: You continue to amaze and support us. From day one, when we mentioned our idea for this book, you enthusiastically encouraged us to send the proposal. Once accepted, you trusted our instincts, challenged our assumptions, and believed in our commitment to make the deadline. Thank you for your faith and your professionalism.

We remain forever grateful for the openness and enthusiasm of the executives we interviewed and visited for our case studies. Thank you, in particular, Lauren St. John at VanCity Credit Union, Bill Wolf at Midway Plumbing, Thomas Kaney at Smith-Kline Beecham, and Norm Snell at Cisco Systems, for your time, willingness, and trust in allowing us free rein in describing your great cultures.

Additionally, we thank all those who were kind enough to offer their personal and professional insights. We particularly appreciate our current and past clients, who, over the years, have given us the seed of ideas and the inspiration to put these truths into book form. You know who you are, and we appreciate your current (and future?) work.

Always saving the best for last, we can never thank enough

our wonderful spouses, Brenda Harris and Michael Brannick, for their unending patience, support, and copy editing. See, we told you we were making progress! Finally, Jim wants to thank his faithful dog, Shamus, whose ceaseless devotion for more than sixteen years continues to soothe his soul.

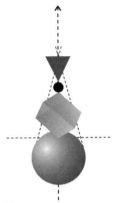

PART ONE

THE POWER OF FOCUS

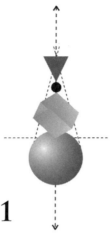

CHAPTER 1

THE GREAT CHALLENGE

"The danger for Corporate America is that the [employee] disconnect . . . sap[s] productivity."

—*BusinessWeek*, June 22, 1998

Everywhere we turn, we hear it.

Why can't I seem to attract more top talent?

Where are all the good employees?

Where can I find them?

And what can I do to keep the great employees I've already got?

The search for great employees has reached an unprecedented level. The labor shortage is now regularly cited as the major deterrent to organizational success and future growth. CEOs and leaders in virtually every industry cry out for more skilled workers. Strategic plans fail, and expansion opportunities are dropped, for lack of manpower. What was once a seemingly endless number of potential employees has become a narrow number of applicants. Furthermore, these few applicants seldom seem to possess the skill level necessary for job success.

With today's unlimited array of tools and resources, it should be easier than ever for companies to find and keep top talent. The explosive growth of executive-search and temporary-help firms, combined with Internet sourcing, brings us in touch with thousands of potential candidates not previously within our reach. Signing bonuses, liberal moving allowances, and spouse job-search assistance are now common staffing activities. Organizations are likewise turning to such creative retention programs as flexible benefits, stay-on bonuses, and stock options. Yet we still struggle to find and keep great employees.

THE CYCLE OF DISCONNECTION

The decades of the 1980s and 1990s have been the most turbulent in business history. Large-scale downsizings, mergers, and acquisitions have reshaped the once traditional long-term connection between company and employee. Radical technological advances in combination with the globalization of commerce have fueled demand for new, higher-level job skills in virtually all industries. The ever-increasing pressure to work longer, faster, and harder has driven millions of workers not only to question their personal commitment to an all-consuming career but to search for meaning outside of the workplace. These are not entirely new phenomena, but in the last two decades, the combined power of these changes have forever altered the once-strong connection between a company and its employees.

The cumulative effect of this workplace turbulence is a disconnected workforce. When, according to the Bureau of Labor Statistics, a typical American holds more than eight different jobs between the ages of 18 and 32, long-term connection to any one company or career is rare. Today's career turmoil has left many workers scarred, scared, and perpetually looking out for themselves rather than the long-term interests. As one professional told *The Wall Street Journal,* "I never stop job hunting."

Employees disconnect on three levels: company, job, and personal. To find and keep outstanding employees, organizations must overcome this growing chasm of disconnection or risk their long-term competitive advantage.

Company Disconnection

Statistics clearly support the conclusion that employees feel a lack of connection to their companies. AT&T recently announced that it desires to cut 11,000 managers by the end of 1999 through a voluntary retirement package. Yet, more than 14,000 managers and employees are now expected to take up such offers.[1] Aon Consulting, a unit of the Chicago-based Aon Insurance company, found that 55 percent of workers said they would switch jobs for a pay increase of 20 percent or less. Additionally, a 1998 survey conducted by Lou Harris and Associates found that 53 percent of U.S. workers expect to voluntarily leave their jobs in the next five years.[2]

Mergers and Acquisitions

Without question, one of the major reasons today's employees disconnect with their companies is that they fear job loss owing to the uncertainty and instability associated with mergers, acquisitions, and downsizings. It seems almost every company today is either reorganizing or contemplating a merger or acquisition. We read every day of the latest megamergers among the Fortune 500, yet some of the most significant mergers are occur-

ring well under the scan of the Wall Street radar screen— among
mainstream America's traditional mom-and-pop businesses.
Consolidators are rapidly buying small, independent, and
family-owned businesses such as funeral homes, plumbing contractors, and real estate offices, organizing them under one administrative umbrella and changing the very face of small
business.

The economies of scale achieved during reorganization,
merger, and consolidation have one inevitable result: job loss.
Workers live in constant fear that their job might be the next
one eliminated. The relentless uncertainty of potential job loss
increases disconnection from the company.

Changing Corporate Focus

Another force that disconnects employees from their companies is management's ever-changing corporate focus. In their
misguided efforts to gain competitive advantage, managers
search for the latest Holy Grail, following the hottest business
guru's advice by introducing yet another corporate initiative.
One month it's service, the next month it's quality, and next
quarter it's employee relations. Employees come to question the
credibility of management and the focus of the company. They
wonder what the company stands for, where it's going, and if
the latest initiative is yet another here today, gone tomorrow
program. Employees are therefore skeptical at best—and cynical
at worst—about their company's perpetually shifting focus.
Without a constant, long-term core focus, organizations con-
fuse, bewilder, depress, and disconnect both potential and actual
employees.

Job Disconnection

The primary reason employees disconnect from their jobs,
though, is that today the jobs themselves are changing cease-

lessly. Competition has forced companies to quickly change markets and products, and thus the jobs that produce them. Position titles, descriptions, and responsibilities change overnight. New technologies require a never-ending upgrade of job skills. Further, downsizings and hiring freezes force employees to wear multiple job hats. Together, these changes create a radical new job reality: *occupational half-life*.

Occupational Half-Life

Every so many years, literally one-half of your current job knowledge and skills become outdated or obsolete. For example, the occupational half-life in 1970 was estimated at somewhere between twelve and fifteen years. This means that by 1985, 50 percent of knowledge and skills an employee had in her job in 1970 had become outdated, even obsolete. Frighteningly, according to the federal Department of Labor, today's best estimates of occupational half-life are in the range of *thirty to thirty-six months*. A constantly changing job combined with a constantly eroding skills base leaves employees feeling more disconnected from their jobs than ever.

The Job and the Core Business

A second reason why employees disconnect from their jobs is that organizations seldom provide a clear link between the job and the core business purpose. Within an environment of ever-changing focus, employees find it hard to keep in sight a strong link between their role and the company's core purpose. Without a strong link, companies primarily rely upon the latest experiment in bonus or short-term incentive programs to motivate employees and find themselves in a bidding war for top talent.

What was once a powerful company connection for many employees—a stable job with a future—has given way to an ever-changing and unpredictable job world. Faced with the reality of job requirements in flux and the weak link between the job and the core business purpose, employees long for a new connection to the company.

Personal Disconnection

As a result of the company and job disconnections, workers today experience a deep personal workplace disconnection as well.

More Than a Paycheck

A driving force behind today's personal disconnection is that today's employees are searching for something more than a paycheck from their work. The baby-boomer generation—those 76 million people born between 1945 and 1964—began their careers under the de facto guarantee of lifetime employment. They have, unfortunately, taken the brunt of today's downsizings and reorganizations and are reexamining their work and life legacies. The baby-buster generation—the 65 million people born between 1965 and 1984—have seen their baby-boomer parents repeatedly outplaced and downsized. Realizing that a lifetime job guarantee is all but dead, they too are looking for a deeper sense of personal connection to something larger than themselves. Unable to find this connection at work, both generations are seeking such connections outside of work.

Voluntary Simplicity—at Work

Employees today are embracing the concept of *voluntary simplicity* to fill the chasm of personal workplace disconnection. Voluntary simplicity is clearly understood when a person voluntarily simplifies his personal life. But what does voluntary simplicity at work include? Going from full-time to part-time, perhaps. Or refusing to relocate, or turning down a promotion to become a supervisor or manager because it would complicate life (regardless of increased income). Nonwork examples of voluntary simplicity that are loosely related to work often center upon time: moving into a townhouse to cut back on yard work and maintenance, relocating to a smaller town with a slower lifestyle, or significantly reducing the amount of time for volunteering with outside groups and causes.

For millions of American workers, putting the career first while robustly pursuing the bottom line has been replaced with putting the family/personal life first while robustly pursuing a better quality of life. The fast track we relished just a few years ago has lost its luster. After years of rising through the ranks, many employees pause and ask, "Is this all there is?" and, in many cases, they don't like the answer.

The fast track often forces an employee's personal life to take a backseat. More and more workers today refuse to allow this to continue. Rather than worry about how their personal life affects their work, employees today are more concerned with how their work affects their personal life. Any aspect of the job that negatively affects their personal life breeds potential personal disconnection. Yet, as all business becomes increasingly competitive, and companies ask even *more* of their workers, personal disconnection will increase.

RENEWING THE CONNECTION

Renewing the connection in finding and keeping great employees is to stop the cycle of disconnection by introducing a new, stable employer-employee connection above and beyond connectedness to the company and the job. Organizations need to give employees a deeper, unchanging reason for the company's existence and the employees' success. Employees need to feel connected to something more permanent and ennobling than a company logo or job title.

> Employees need to feel connected to something more permanent and ennobling than a company logo or job title.

If organizations continue to embrace traditional approaches to finding and keeping top talent (such as generous pay, benefits, and personal time), they perpetuate the cycle of disconnection while diminishing their ultimate productivity and profit.

NOTES

1. *BusinessWeek* (June 15, 1998), p. 53.
2. *St. Petersburg Times* (February 8, 1998).

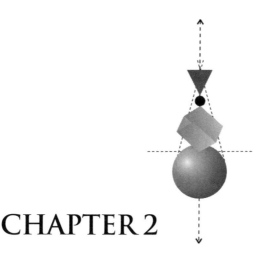

CHAPTER 2

THE CULTURE CONNECTION

"Our culture is our competitive advantage."

—Mike Smith, CEO, Lands' End

A popular TV commercial opens with a manager for a large office products company reviewing a huge manual of the latest product price reductions. As he hands the telephone-sized book to a frontline clerk and instructs the clerk to retag all the listed items before leaving the store, the clerk pauses only briefly before exuberantly shouting "All right!" and beginning a dance of joy around the store. The manager smiles and walks away, saying, "That kid was a find!"

What inspires the clerk to want to stay late and retag hundreds of items? What makes him shout for joy rather than jam the pricing gun down the manager's throat? How has the manager found and retained such an apparently enthusiastic employee? Either by luck or design, the manager has bridged with this employee the missing link in today's staffing and retention challenge.

THE MISSING LINK

The evidence is clear, and experts agree:

- ▼ James Collins and Jerry Porras, in their best-selling book *Built to Last*, state that an essential ingredient of all excellent organizations is their "core ideology"; "the point is to build an organization that fervently preserves its core ideology in specific, concrete ways."[1]
- ▼ In their landmark book *Corporate Cultures*, Terrence Deal and Allan Kennedy conclude that a strong culture "enables people to feel better about what they do."[2]
- ▼ According to the *Fuqua Report,* the top two reasons people join a company are the opportunity for personal growth and the culture; core culture is the key driver of individual growth.[3]
- ▼ Noted human resource and retention expert Jack Fitzenz has found that the two reasons why most people leave a company are the supervisor and the culture; it is the culture that drives the ultimate relationship with the supervisor.
- ▼ Norm Snell, director of global compensation and benefits for Cisco Systems, fervently believes that a company "can only tinker with compensations and benefits systems so much; it's culture, culture, culture"[4] that must drive staffing and retention systems.
- ▼ John Kotter and James Heskett conclude that corporate culture "may even be greater than all those factors that

have been discussed most often in the organizational and business literature—strategy, organizational structure, management systems, financial analysis tools, leadership, etc."[5]

▼ "The relationship we have with our people and the culture of our company is our most sustainable competitive advantage," says Howard Schultz, the founder of Starbucks.[6]

The missing link in today's search to find and keep great employees is to align staffing and retention activities to the company's core culture. Aligned companies break out of the cycle of disconnection and find and keep top-notch employees through a laser-like focus on their core culture. They recognize that they need to build a strong, stable, and lasting consciousness of connection for both prospective and current employees. Aligning their staffing and retention processes to core culture is their preferred method of driving long-term organization success.

> Aligned companies break out of the cycle of disconnection and find and keep top-notch employees through a laserlike focus on their core culture.

THE FOUR CORE CULTURES

Aligned companies base their staffing and retention processes upon one of four forms of core culture.

Customer Service

The underlying purpose of a customer-service culture is to create customer solutions. Competitive advantage is gained through getting close to the customer. These companies strive to think as their customers do, anticipate their needs, and create value for them. Customer-service cultures often empower the frontline service worker, and create strong customer-employee partnership links that build high levels of repeat business.

Innovation

A second core culture is that of innovation. The underlying purpose of an innovation culture is to create the future. Competitive advantage comes from unleashing the power of technology to create new products, new markets, and new niches within existing markets. Their voracious appetite for brainpower is matched only by an innovation culture's appetite for staying on the cutting edge.

Operational Excellence

The third core culture is operational excellence. The underlying purpose of an operationally excellent culture is to create a process that minimizes costs while maximizing productivity and efficiency. Competitive advantage is in attaining process excellence from product or service creation and delivery. The foundation of an operationally excellent culture is to constantly improve systems, procedures, and product or service quality.

Spirit

The fastest-growing core culture is spirit. The underlying purpose of a culture of spirit is to create an environment that inspires employee excellence. Competitive advantage is gained through unleashing people's limitless energy, creativity, and enthusiasm. Spirit-driven cultures often embrace a higher-order purpose, a corporate goal that stretches toward a greater common good. They capitalize on the collective energy and spirit of their people to propel them to excellence.

Culture and Financial Performance

Note that financial performance is not a core culture. Financial performance is a result or an outcome, not a driver, of organizational excellence. Companies that claim they are "financially driven" are simply reversing the true sequence of outcome (for example, profit or shareholder value) from goal (outstanding customer service, innovation, operational excellence, or employee spirit). A deeper look inside such companies shows that typically one of the four core cultures is the preferred vehicle toward financial success. Further, Bill Wiggenhorn, president of Motorola University, reminds us that unless you are a member of the executive committee, "'Shareholder equity Rah! Rah! Rah!' just doesn't get people out of bed each day."[7]

> Financial performance is a result or an outcome, not a driver, of organizational excellence.

SEPARATE BUT EQUAL

The four core cultures are separate but equal. No one core culture is superior to another. None is more likely to guarantee outstanding financial performance than another. All are equally powerful in driving long-term organizational success.

In most companies, elements of all four cultures exist simultaneously. Without question, customer service, innovation, operational excellence, and employee spirit are all important. But to find and keep great employees, key questions must be asked and answered:

▼ Which one core culture is most important to your company?

▼ Which single core culture sustains the pure essence of your success?

▼ Which core culture affords the best route to your company's competitive advantage?

The key to finding and keeping excellent employees, therefore, is to align your staffing and retention to the one core culture that best propels your company's success.

THE BENEFITS OF ALIGNMENT

You enjoy numerous benefits when you align staffing and retention processes to core culture.

▼ *Alignment is strategic.* Aligned companies build focused, long-term staffing and retention practices that drive the core culture. Staffing and retention functions therefore are strong strategic partners that help build business success. Processes are based upon the core culture and judged on the ability to maintain competitive advantage. Nonaligned companies are reactive, continually shifting their focus and implementing tactical programs with little or no direct correlation to core business success.

▼ *Alignment simplifies the staffing and retention process.* Selection and retention decisions are far simpler within an aligned company. Staffing and retention initiatives are created from the core culture. Selection, promotion, and retention decisions focus on maintaining a culturally aligned workforce. Nonaligned companies often have confusing, convoluted programs designed around several, or all four, core cultures. Selection, promotion, and retention decisions become confusing and complicated.

▼ *Alignment strengthens the core culture.* Since staffing and retention are based upon core culture, decisions reached within aligned companies perpetually strengthen the core culture. Without a core-culture focus, nonaligned companies make decisions in relative isolation from understanding core business purpose; thus they perpetuate a more convoluted culture.

▼ *Alignment builds strong company connections.* Applicants and employees grasp that there is a focused, consistent purpose throughout the staffing and retention processes. Even within today's environment of manic reorganizations and mergers, aligned companies generate a new, stable connectedness having core culture rather than lifetime employment as its basis. Nonaligned companies, especially when faced with reorganizations or mergers, continue to disconnect people from their employers as they ignore the opportunity to build new connections to core culture.

▼ *Alignment builds strong job connections.* Aligned companies connect every job to its context and how the job strengthens the core culture. Applicants and current employees therefore feel linked to all of the company's jobs by way of participation in the core culture. Thus individual job staffing and retention decisions are based on more than generic personality characteristics; they focus on which characteristics best sustain the core culture. Nonaligned companies rely too heavily upon job skills, ignoring the cultural context of the job and its pervasive impact on the employee's success on the job.

▼ *Alignment builds strong personal connections.* Aligned companies help bridge the disconnection gap that troubles excellent employees, like the one who told *Fortune* magazine she was "tired of working incredibly hard for companies that . . . didn't share my values."[8] The focus on core culture helps aligned companies satisfy employees' deeper need to make a difference on connection to personal values. It is also easier at aligned compa-

nies to show how candidates and employees can make a difference in promoting the core culture, which is a more satisfying
personal connection than any signing or retention bonus could
ever deliver. Employees within aligned companies think twice
about leaving, for fear of losing the special personal connection.
Nonaligned companies continue to fight the selfish side of
what's-in-it-for-me (among both candidates and current employees). Without building new connections, nonaligned companies rely far too heavily on money-driven practices in their
attempts to find and keep valuable employees. Such employees
are harder to retain because they often feel compelled to search
for new opportunities and stronger personal connections to
their work and their employer.

▼ *The ultimate benefit is a unique competitive advantage:
the ability to consistently find and keep top talent.* With staffing
and retention processes based upon their core culture, an aligned
company attracts and retains far more superior employees that
fit well with its core culture than a nonaligned company does.
High productivity can be directly attributed to a focused, concerted plan to align staffing and retention practices to the core
culture. With no clear focus for their staffing and retention, nonaligned companies suffer greater disconnections throughout
their organizations. Staffing and retention becomes a burden
rather than a competitive advantage.

In summary, aligned and nonaligned companies differ
markedly in the nature of their staffing and retention processes:

Aligned Companies	*Nonaligned Companies*
Processes are strategic.	Processes are reactive.
Simplify pursuit of business goals.	Complicate pursuit of business goals.
Strengthen the core culture.	Convolute the culture.

Build company connections.	Promote company disconnections.
Build job connections.	Promote job disconnections.
Build personal connections.	Amount to competitive disadvantage.
Afford competitive advantage.	

THE PROCESS OF ALIGNMENT

There are three steps to the process of alignment:

1. The organization must clearly understand how each core culture uniquely contributes to employee connectedness.
2. The organization must embrace one core culture as its operational driver.
3. Management must then align all staffing and retention strategies to the core culture.

Does the focus on one core culture totally eliminate all your staffing and retention problems? Does it automatically attract thousands of superior employee applicants or transform all the average performers into great employees? No, of course not. No one formula can ever produce such results. We are not prescribing a magic pill that forever eliminates your staffing and retention challenges. Rather, in this book we outline a method in use at leading companies that keeps them one step ahead of their competition. Through their efforts to carefully align staffing and retention to their core culture, they attract and retain a high-performing employees at a rate that is the envy of their competitors. This is the distinct competitive advantage: being an organization filled with culturally aligned and motivationally connected employees.

Now, it's your turn to build a competitive advantage for your organization based upon one of four core cultures.

NOTES

1. James Collins and Jerry Porras, *Built to Last: Successful Habits of Visionary Companies* (New York: HarperBusiness, 1994), p. 135.

2. Terrence E. Deal and Alan Kennedy, *Corporate Cultures: The Rites and Rituals of Corporate Life* (Reading, Mass.: Addison-Wesley, 1982), pp. 15–16.

3. *The Fuqua Report* (May 16, 1998).

4. Telephone interview (March 10, 1998).

5. John P. Kotter and James L. Heskett, *Corporate Culture and Performance* (New York: The Free Press, 1992), p. 9.

6. "Caffeine Nation," *Human Resource Executive* (March 1996), p. 28.

7. Jim Harris, *Getting Employees to Fall in Love With Your Company* (New York: AMACOM, 1996), p. 21.

8. Daniel Pink, "Free Agent Nation," *Fast Company* (December-January) 1998, pp. 131–147.

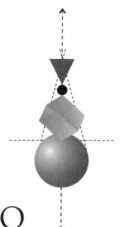

PART TWO

THE FOUR CORE CULTURES

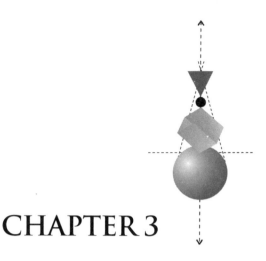

CHAPTER 3

A CULTURE OF CUSTOMER SERVICE

"Our customers are everything. Without them, nothing else matters."

—The Customer Creed at Office Depot

Just about every company's mission or values statement promises outstanding customer service, but few companies actually deliver on the promise. We can all think of examples of companies that deliver great service: Nordstrom, Home Depot, Ritz-Carlton, and Walt Disney World. Each has created and sustained its success through commitment to a culture that sets the standard for providing superb customer service.

A CULTURE THAT SOLVES PROBLEMS

The underlying purpose of a customer-service culture is to create solutions to meet customer needs. As we suggested in defining the customer-service core culture in Chapter 2, competitive advantage here is in knowing and thinking like the customers, meeting their current and future needs, and creating value for them using every means at one's disposal.

> Competitive advantage is in knowing and thinking like the customers, meeting their current and future needs, and creating value for them using every means at one's disposal.

Creating solutions and providing values are the cornerstones upon which companies with a culture of customer service are built. These companies invest a significant amount of time, labor, energy, and money in providing their employees with the tools, resources, and training necessary to deliver exemplary service. The thought of providing only mediocre, we're-as-good-as-everyone-else service is abhorrent to world-class, service-driven organizations. Every employee within these companies, from the CEO to the frontline service provider, sees the connection between her job and the company's goal of providing outstanding customer service.

The core cultural values of innovation, quality, and employee spirit are, of course, important to organizations with a focused customer-service culture. Yet being customer-service-driven remains supreme. With a foundation of service excellence:

1. Innovation increases as employees focus on anticipating customer needs and developing new and better ways to meet those needs.
2. Quality increases through each employee's commitment to provide outstanding customer service.
3. Employee satisfaction increases as each person under-

stands the critical role he or she plays in helping the company achieves its customer-service goals.

Companies with customer-service cultures empower the frontline service worker. Why? Only through an empowered front line can service-driven cultures create the lasting partnership links between employee and customer that build high levels of repeat business. Moreover, customer-service-driven cultures build customer links beyond the front line and into virtually all operations, by way of feedback loops, face-to-face interactions, customer survey activities, and the like.

Customer Service Equals Customer Solution

Customer-service cultures go beyond providing only a product or service to their customers; they provide solutions. They recognize that today's consumer needs more than just low price (although low price is a good thing) and more than just great selection (although great selection is also good). Today's customer needs answers, alternatives, and solutions to unique problems.

Employee Training

Home Depot is a prime example of a customer-service–driven culture that views service in terms of solutions. Beginning at the point of sale, Home Depot offers a full range of product knowledge training programs for employees. The first week in the store, all new hires must complete a product knowledge workbook on their department. Within thirty days of being hired, employees complete the product knowledge books for other departments. All employees are encouraged to complete all the product knowledge books and be awarded the "product knowledge master" award, a badge in the design of a cap and gown to be worn on their aprons.

Customer Training

Home Depot also provides training for customers on how to use the products. Proudly displayed during a recent visit to my neighborhood Home Depot in Tampa were announcements of special upcoming workshops on how to install wood laminate flooring, how to replace bathroom tile, and how to hang wallpaper—every one of them meant to give customers face-to-face solutions rather than merely to sell product. The store even sponsors workshops for customers' kids!

Using Creative Solutions

Another example further demonstrates Home Depot's customer-service-as-customer-solution philosophy. Recently, I was searching for a solution to a pesky problem: Squirrels were eating all the food from my bird feeder. I approached a Home Depot associate and proudly explained a well-thought-out (but somewhat costly) solution I had come up with. Rather than selling me the equipment I thought I needed, the associate told me to take along—at no charge—a less-expensive material that would be far easier to implement to solve my problem. Not only did I avoid having to purchase things I did not really need, but I received a customized solution just for the asking!

Home Depot's CEO, Arthur Blank, says he loves to hear stories of how associates save customers money through creative solutions rather than gouging them with products they may not need.

Viewing customer service as an opportunity to provide solutions is one thing that separates world-class customer-service cultures from the rest. Customer-service-driven cultures like that of Home Depot continuously create solutions for all their customers.

A Step Ahead

A significant defining factor of cultures driven by service excellence is their passion for a proactive rather than reactive approach to serving the customer. They realize that to stay ahead of the *competition* and truly live their commitment to customer service, they need to stay one step ahead of the *customer*.

According to John Graham, author of *Magnet Marketing*, a new definition of customer service is emerging. His definition goes beyond the standard protocol of doing it right the first time, or providing communication excellence, or making on-time deliveries, or being responsive to individual customer requirements. These actions are simply starting points for service. If customers do not receive this level of service, it is a given that they will go somewhere else. Graham suggests that customer service for the future requires that companies become a valuable resource for the customer.[1] To do this, customer service companies need to know their customers better than the customers know themselves.

A good example of a company staying a step ahead of its customers is New England Business Service (NEBS) of Groton, Massachusetts. NEBS is a leading office-products and business-forms supplier in the Northeast. Realizing that occasionally some of their forms and supplies may be damaged during delivery, NEBS anticipates the customers' response to that occurrence by offering free replacements. During the recent El Niño storms, which damaged many packages, NEBS mailed a letter to all customers announcing the free-replacement offer and giving a toll-free phone number for ease of reordering. The offer was good for six months, and NEBS also provided a billing-cycle extension for the disaster-stricken business that might be low on cash.[2]

Knowing your customer sometimes means knowing that all customers are not the same. This message of not-one-size-fits-all is even being heard within religious denominations. Many churches are becoming more "customer friendly" in their approach to serving their communities. Whether conducting church services with contemporary, upbeat music and spiced with live drama, art, and skits or minimizing the presence of traditional religious symbols and decor, religious groups all across the country are discovering a huge new "customer base" through sensitivity to the fact that all customers are not alike.

CORE-CULTURE CONNECTIONS

Customer-driven cultures connect to employees in many interesting ways.

Reach Out and Touch

In companies with a culture of customer service, *every* employee is connected to the customer. The message of service excellence goes far beyond the frontline employee who has the most frequent customer contact. In companies that best exemplify a customer-service-driven culture, senior and midlevel managers routinely meet with and interact with clients, production employees go to the customer site to better understand how the product is used, and all employees are responsible for addressing requests from customers.

> In companies with a culture of customer service, *every* employee is connected to the customer.

We recently observed a fine example of how even senior executives take a hands-on, walk-the-talk approach to inspiring service excellence. While waiting in the gate area for a Saturday morning departing flight, we recognized Robert Crandall, then CEO of American Airlines, at a nearby gate. Crandall was carefully listening to an American Airlines employee when a customer approached the pair and asked a question. Both of them responded to the customer inquiry, with Crandall taking down several notes on what the passenger was saying during the course of the conversation.

We doubt if the customer knew she was talking to the CEO of American Airlines, but it doesn't matter. Crandall was clearly interested in what the customer had to say and would apparently take that customer's information back to the relevant department at American to address the issue. His goal was not just to address the problem for that customer but to make an effort for all customers to benefit from that one exchange. Employees who work for companies with customer-service cultures create new opportunities, and take advantage of existing ones, to reach out and touch the customer, regardless of their level or position within the company.

The Customer Is Always the Customer

Perhaps the most flak (as well as the most fun) I have experienced as feedback on my first book, *Getting Employees to Fall in Love With Your Company* (AMACOM, 1997), resulted from the somewhat radical notion of allowing frontline employees input into "firing" customers. By this, I mean that all companies have customers that are irritating, irrational, or impossible to please. These customers cost the company and employees more time, energy, and money than they are worth. Ultimately, these customers take valuable resources away from more valuable customers. Customers who strongly support a culture of customer service need to "fire" customers who are more trouble than they are worth so that they can best meet their current and future customer service needs. This notion flies in the face of the conventional wisdom that the customer is always right. Whether you believe the customer is or isn't always right, one thing all service-driven companies agree upon is that the customer is always *the customer,* and that, right or wrong, it is everyone's job to deliver outstanding service to that source of all business.

Companies resist the idea of firing the customer because, on the surface, it appears to violate every principle associated with providing outstanding customer service. On the other hand, customer service is a two-way relationship that involves the customer and the employee who is providing the service. Top companies clearly communicate their performance standard to employees who are responsible for serving the customer. These companies are also just as clear regarding customer behavior. Customers not living up to the company's expectations are sometimes asked to take their business elsewhere.

Although allowing customers to be fired is not a universally accepted practice within all customer-service cultures, it is gaining popularity. It allows these companies to lavish even more time and world-class service on core customers, as well as imposing even higher standards of service that decrease the likelihood of any customer needing to be fired. By clearly defining employee and customer expectations and acting on those expectations, the prospect of firing a customer sends a message to employees and customers alike about which performance standards are acceptable and which are unacceptable.

Love and Marriage

In love and marriage, a defining characteristic of a successful relationship is putting the needs of the other person above your own. Companies that embody the spirit of customer service practice this same principle with their customers. They often put their customers' needs ahead of the company needs. By doing so, these companies build long-term relationships and extreme loyalty from core customers who know that they truly do come first.

Ryder, the Florida-based transportation services company, provides a strong example of a company that truly puts customer needs first. Companies frequently contract with Ryder to deliver their goods. As part of this service, Ryder's drivers often wear the uniforms of the client companies. This is a win-win situation for Ryder and its customers. The Ryder customer is better served because the customer's name remains in front of the ultimate customer. In turn, Ryder gains long-term business and extreme loyalty because its customers see a tangible sign of Ryder's commitment to serving them—a sign that clearly shows Ryder putting the customer's image needs above its own.

Another company that practices the notion of love and marriage in its daily operations is PeopleSoft, a Pleasanton, California–based developer of enterprise-side application software. PeopleSoft organizes its operations around customers rather than products or sales. More than 300 account managers are the customer's primary point of contact and act as liaison between the customer and other divisions of the company. The account manager and the contact person within the customer organization are extremely close because of the frequent contact with and the varied responsibilities of the account manager; it's not unusual for a customer to become dependent on an account manager. Whenever an account manager is relocated or gets promoted, he is responsible for ensuring a smooth transition in the customer's relationship with the new account manager. To support this relationship, account managers at PeopleSoft are not commissioned sales staff, which is common practice. Rather than being rewarded on sales performance, account managers at PeopleSoft are rewarded according to how easy it is for custom-

ers to implement the company's software, and for overall customer satisfaction. Customers routinely experience such great
comfort with their account managers that they see them as part
of their company rather than PeopleSoft employees.

"I Own the Problem"

In her book *Fabled Service*, Betsy Sanders says it is no longer
enough to have well-meaning, very nice people attending to customers' needs. The key to outstanding service is enabling those
people to deliver the highest-quality product or service at the
very best price. Although merely good customer service focuses
on friendliness and courtesy, outstanding service focuses on execution and satisfaction—execution by employees who take real
ownership of the customer situation, which in turn increases
customer satisfaction.[3]

Companies with a true customer-service culture embrace
the concept that an employee who hears a customer problem
"owns" the customer problem. Great service is delivered when
empowered frontline employees are given the freedom to address and correct customer complaints or problems themselves,
instead of having to hand the customer off to a manager or to
another department in the company. Such companies reward
employees who solve customers' problems regardless of their
position or level within the organization. Many nonaligned
companies believe that entrusting frontline employees is at best
naïve, and at worst just plain stupid. Great customer-service-
driven cultures, however, realize that world-class service can
only result from employees' being empowered and willing to
own the customer's problem.

> Great service is delivered when empowered frontline
> employees are given the freedom to address and correct
> customer complaints or problems themselves.

To own a customer's problem, employees must have both the desire and the authority to take action. Without the desire, no amount of authority convinces an employee to own the problem. Without enough authority to act, no amount of personal motivation can overcome the frustration of wanting to take care of the customer but not being given the freedom to do so.

Genuine customer-service cultures create environments that allow employees to own the problems. Nordstrom, the Seattle-based department store chain, is famous for allowing its employees the freedom to solve customer problems. The company's now-famous employee policy states:

Rule Number 1: Use your good judgment in all situations.
Rule Number 2: There will be no additional rules.

Throughout Nordstrom, inspired employees enthusiastically own customer problems because management allows them the freedom to succeed.

Perhaps the most annoying example of employees' not being given the freedom to own the customer's problem is the still common (and dreaded) call for a price check. (This problem is annoying because the customer's problem was actually created by the store.) Frustrated cashiers frustrate other employees who are summoned to run off and find the price for an article, all the while frustrating everyone else in line. At Target department stores, if an item's price does not display on the register, the cashier is trained to ask the customer if she remembers the price of the item. If the customer's price sounds reasonable to the cashier, he rings it up. Target's customer-service culture empowers the frontline to own and immediately respond to the customer's problem.

The first service company to win the coveted Malcolm Baldrige award, the Ritz-Carlton hotel chain, takes owning the customer's problem to new heights. Employees are authorized to invest cash—up to $2,000, on the spot—to do anything they need to do to rectify a guest's complaint (e.g., unsatisfactory room accommodations, lost dry-cleaning, car scratched in hotel parking lot).[4] The unmatched spirit of service received at any Ritz-Carlton is in part due to the company's incredible encouragement for any employee to take ownership of any customer problem and fix it—now!

Real-Time Reactions

In today's fast-paced business world, anything less than an immediate reaction to customer needs is too slow. Every organization receives real-time reactions from customers. Some businesses use the feedback to help make decisions on service improvement, while others simply ignore the feedback. But within a service-driven culture, fast, focused, and direct reactions to customer feedback are a defining force for success. It is critical to the sustained success of any customer-service culture to deliver immediate, direct customer solutions or else face losing business. Customers walk away if they don't get unique, customized solutions to their problems. Any company able to carry out quickly such responses continues to reap the benefits of long-term repeat business. Thanks to effective, real-time reactions to customers, service-driven cultures maintain their competitive edge because their core cultural purpose prompts the response that the customer needs.

Additionally, service cultures benefit as the same real-time reactions serve employees in their individual role of ultimately solving the needs of customers. Real-time reactions reinforce to frontline service employees when they are on track and when they are not. Often the feedback is as simple as an employee receiving a big smile or hearing a simple thank-you from the boss. Sometimes the feedback takes the form of a daily review of the employee's strengths and areas in which service delivery can be improved. In either case, such real-time reactions to employees create the foundation from which world-class, service-driven cultures maintain their unique competitive edge.

Beyond these obvious cases for customer-contact employees, service-driven cultures use real-time reactions to improve behind-the-scenes processes and systems that involve literally every employee. From vendor accounting procedures to distribution channels, from inventory management systems to product packaging, service-driven cultures integrate real-time reactions into the very fabric of their companies.

Great employees within service-driven cultures strongly connect to the practice of real-time reactions. Driven by their own need to stay a step ahead and create customer solutions, superior employees connect with organizations whose processes and systems support their passionate efforts to achieve world-class service. It is through integrating real-time reactions into the core processes of an organization that customer-service cultures create strong connections for first-rate employees.

Midway Services: Above and Beyond

You answer the knock at your front door. As you open it, you glance at a freshly washed and beautifully painted van parked out front. Standing at your door is a clean-cut, uniformed, professional-looking person. After greeting you with a friendly "Good morning," the professional asks, "May I enter your house?" As you answer yes, the professional then pulls on a pair of surgical-style booties over shined black work shoes before entering your home. There follow a careful inspection and from a superbly printed catalog before any work begins. If you agree to the work, a red carpet is then placed under the work area to protect the floor. In the end, the work area is left cleaner than when the work began.

Who would you say is at the front door? An upscale builder of custom homes conducting a final interior inspection of your multimillion-dollar home? Perhaps an antiques dealer or restorer estimating repairs for your grandmother's china cabinet?

Well, if you happen to live in west central Florida, you are likely to shout out the correct answer: "Oh—that's my plumber from Midway Services!"

Midway Services is a Clearwater, Florida, plumbing, heating, and air conditioning services company. Midway is a nationally recognized industry leader and frequent award winner whose 140-some employees generate more than $10 million in sales by providing cutting-edge customer service to homeowners, builders, and remodelers in the area. Within an industry dominated by small mom-and-pop shops, Midway Services continues to be one of the largest and fastest growing companies of its type in America. Its success stems from an industry-unique customer-service culture.

Service Above and Beyond

A few years ago, Midway's president, Bill Wolf, was looking for a unique marketing approach that would epitomize the company's customer-service philosophy of "above and beyond." He wanted to create an indelible, lasting, and positive impression on his customers and the community. Wolf's marketing team purchased an inventor's remote-control blimp, twenty-six feet long and eight feet in diameter. They painted it with the Midway Services logo and began flying over Tampa Bay Buccaneer games, Christmas parades, and local high school events. Midway's airship is a brilliant representation of its above-and-beyond customer-service philosophy.

Midway embraces a total customer solution. The goal is to retain lifetime customers, not one-time in-and-out jobs; the first job is an opportunity to build a long-term relationship for all of the customer's plumbing, electric, and air conditioning needs.

The customer's perception of total value is critical to Midway. Whereas most of Midway's competitors rush through repairs in a hurry to get to their next call, Midway's service technicians invest a little extra time with each customer. The service technician, conducting a walk-through inspection alongside the customer, examines the customer's entire plumbing, electric, and air conditioning systems, explaining each system's functions while answering questions and uncovering additional service opportunities. Service technicians also take the time to carefully explain every item on the bill, ensuring that the customer understands the value-added of each activity.

Customer response is so positive to this hands-on personalized service that more often than not when additional services opportunities are uncovered, the customer agrees to the additional repairs on the spot. Along with its industry-leading flat-rate pricing structure (one price—no surprises), this level of customer service and customer perception of value soar above and beyond the competition.

Black Belts, Black Shoes, a Haircut, and a Shave

Midway clearly understands that to deliver superior customer service, technicians often have to go the extra mile and graciously submit to the customer's sometimes unusual requests. Midway therefore designs its staffing process around uncovering an employment applicant's willingness to fully serve others. For example, early in the first interview, management tells the applicant that black belts and polishable black shoes are required, as are a haircut and a shave. Within an industry too often characterized by slovenly attired repairpersons who seldom display the desire to yield to a customer's unusual demands, many applicants hesitate or simply refuse to accept these unusual standards. Yet this one simple dictum allows Midway to peek inside the potential employee's "heart for service," while allowing unsuited applicants to graciously deselect themselves from the staffing process.

The Council of Many

In what is called its "council-of-many principle," Midway involves many employees in the staffing process. None are more important, though, than the service technicians themselves. If applicants pass the initial interviews and background screening processes, service technicians take them on service calls. Midway's service technicians watch how the applicant interacts and connects with the customer, observing willingness to do what the customer asks (especially the unusual), a sense of owning the customer's problems, and drive to provide long-term customer solutions. The service technician also judges the applicant's willingness to really go above and beyond by asking her to carry the customer's newspaper in from the street, or change a light bulb, or even bring in the mail. Applicants may accompany several service technicians during the process. Management then relies on the cumulative evaluations of the service technician for the final staffing decision. Midway is looking more for the right person with the right service attitude than for the right technician.

Retention Above and Beyond

In addition to its extensive recruiting processes, Midway goes above and beyond in its desire to retain great employees. Perhaps the most aggravating aspect of life as a plumber, electrician, or air conditioning technician is being on call twenty-four hours a day, seven days a week. To better help longtime technicians have a life outside work, Midway has instituted a simple retention policy that rewards longevity. Any service technician who has five consecutive years of company service is removed from the on-call roster. This one policy alone is a powerful incentive for service technicians to remain with Midway.

Midway's innovative marketing strategy is designed to further reduce the need for emergency and after-hours service calls. Instead of relying upon traditional yellow-pages ads that automatically attract these demanding calls, Midway focuses on building business through routine maintenance service schedules and customer referrals. This insightful combination of policies reduces the number of emergency and after-hours calls as well as increasing uninterrupted evening time even for the on-call technicians. Thus the technicians with less than five years service too benefit from Midway's creation of an environment that maximizes all employees' time with family and friends.

With the same passion as that for serving customers, Midway goes to great lengths to stay a step ahead for service technicians. Repairpersons at other companies may drive a battered van and waste valuable time in restocking their own supplies, but Midway's service technicians are given clean, organized, and regularly reconditioned trucks or vans that are constantly restocked by warehouse workers. Midway believes that providing the same care to technicians as to customers helps retain top employee talent.

Another important element in the retention strategy is continuous customer-service training. Weekly service technician meetings focus on new service concepts and techniques, sharing service success stories, and celebrating positive customer feedback letters and milestones in technicians' careers. An extensive corporate lending library of books, tapes, and videos allows all staff to keep their service-excellence skills current. Additionally, Midway has an audiocassette learning series (which rotates weekly) that allows technicians the opportunity to continue learning during their extensive driving time.

From booties and red carpets to black belts and blimps, Midway Services is a world-class example of a customer-service culture that attracts and keeps great employees.

NOTES

1. John Graham, "Customer Service Redefined: The Game Has Changed Again," www.smartbiz.com/sbs/arts/jrg17.htm (April 27, 1998).

2. "This Month's Winning Customer Service Story," www.therightanswer. html (April 27, 1998).

3. Betsy Sanders, "Ordinary Acts, Extraordinary Outcomes," excerpted from *Fabled Service* by Betsy Sanders (San Francisco: Pfeiffer, 1995), www.smartbiz.com/sbs/arts/ebs1.htm.

4. Jim Harris, *Getting Employees to Fall in Love With Your Company* (New York: AMACOM, 1996).

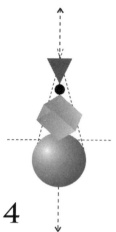

CHAPTER 4

A CULTURE OF INNOVATION

"Let chaos reign; then reign in chaos."

—Andy Grove, Chairman, Intel

In the constant pursuit to create something from nothing, chaos occurs. The seemingly unmanageable nature of chaos repels those personalities who are either faint of heart or consumed with structure and order. Neither person would survive within a culture of innovation. Rightly so, because a culture of innovation by its very nature is on a unique path—one that, unfortunately, few organizations are willing to take.

The underlying purpose of an innovation-driven culture is to create and shape the future. Whether in manufacturing, health care, software development, or consumer goods, cultures of innovation strive not only to bring tomorrow's products and services to market today but also to passionately pursue their unique visions of what the future should be and how their products and services will dominate it.

> The underlying purpose of an innovation-driven culture is to create and shape the future.

Being first to market can be a life-or-death proposition for an innovation-driven company. Considering that the development of a single new drug compound can take fifteen years and $300 million of investment, being first to market in the pharmaceutical industry can mean the difference between getting rich or going broke. In the software business, where competitive advantage is measured in weeks (days?) rather than years, being first to market is a far quicker life or death.

Being first by no means implies flawless performance. There's a popular saying within the pioneering company Cisco Systems: "Being first is not elegant." Yet Cisco's drive to be first has made it one of the world's technologically elite companies.

Just as the ever-popular science fiction series *Star Trek* proclaims, innovation-driven companies "boldly go where no one has gone before." Inherent within this approach is a strong desire to invent the future rather than redesign the past. Even with all its uncertainty, a focus on inventing the future is far more exciting to an innovation-driven company than simply redesigning current systems and processes. Of course, redesign of current systems can be a critical component of organizational success; however, a core driver within cultures of innovation is to be part of creating the future.

Unleashing the power of technology is a primary means to competitive advantage within cultures of innovation. The marvel of the computer chip has opened countless opportunities for a company with a culture of innovation to gain market dominance within virtually any industry. From singing greeting cards to artificial limbs, from satellite-assisted automobile map guidance systems to voice-activated software programs, unleashing technology is an essential element of success within a culture of innovation.

> The marvel of the computer chip has opened countless opportunities for a company with a culture of innovation to gain market dominance within virtually any industry.

Innovation-driven cultures leverage technology, investing massive dollars in research and development to create new, cutting-edge products; looking for ways to expand their unique products or services into new markets; and focusing on ways to proactively exploit new niches within existing markets, tailoring their offerings to individual clients and individual customers.

Innovation cultures have a voracious appetite for brainpower. Never can an innovation-driven culture have enough bright, energetic people around; there is always a desire and need for more. Therefore, innovation-driven cultures are compelled to focus their energies on finding and keeping the intellectual elite, the women and men within the upper quartile of intelligence. A voracious appetite for brainpower within cultures of innovation is matched only by an appetite for staying on the cutting edge. With markets appearing and disappearing overnight, the drive to stay ahead is omnipresent. The pressure to compete, outperform, and win perpetuates the need for arming innovation companies with the latest and greatest technology. Such loaded-to-the-rafters technology not only keeps innovation-driven companies on the cutting edge but also is an absolute mandate to finding and keeping top talent. The reason is simple: The best and brightest people want to play with the best and brightest technology. Without one, you do not get the other.

Innovation-driven cultures are leading the way in what has

become a fascinating change in the corporate pecking order. In most organizations, the three most powerful positions are typically the chief executive officer, followed by the chief operating officer or president, and then the chief financial officer. Since technology has become such a necessary element of success across all types of companies, it is now common to find the company's chief information officer (CIO) replacing the CFO as number three in importance in the corporate hierarchy. Obviously, the CIO has always had a significant role within innovation-driven cultures, but the importance of this role is now beginning to spread into many other organizational structures.

ON THE EDGE OF PARANOIA

Innovation-driven cultures inhabit a world characterized by constant paranoia. They are propelled by constant fear that they could quickly disappear, either through the obsolescence of today's products and services or through the sudden first-to-market appearance of a competitor's product. If general paranoia does not exist in the organization, some leaders create it. Jim Clark, CEO of Netscape, says that one of his primary jobs is to create paranoia, and the title of Andy Grove's best-selling book suggests that *Only the Paranoid Survive*.[1]

Much of the paranoia inside today's innovation-driven cultures stems from the frightening reality of knowledge half-life. To contemplate this is to ask the question, "How long will it take 50 percent of the latest, hot-off-the-press products or services to become obsolete?" Estimates are that the half-life of computer hardware is a mere three years.[2] This means that within three years, one-half of the hardware configuration on your brand-new, high-speed laptop with all its bells and whistles laptop will be obsolete. Take a guess what the estimated half-life of computer software is today. If you guess more than one and a half years, you're wrong. It is frightening to think that half of your current, costly, top-of-the-line software will be outdated within eighteen months. But even more frighteningly, imagine if your *business* is hardware or software development! Is it any wonder that such innovation-driven companies live in constant paranoia?

The key to surviving it, according to world-renowned information technology guru James Martin, is to focus on the external enemy (the competition), not the internal partner.[3] Great care is taken to create an us-versus-them mentality within innovation-driven cultures, a mentality that sustains paranoia about the competition while simultaneously inspiring employees to accept production deadlines that commonly seem impossible to meet. Sensing—or even fabricating—intense attacks from all competitors, innovation-driven companies remain on the edge of paranoia.

COLLECTIVE CRANIUMS

Without question, the number one asset in innovation-driven cultures is brainpower. Any executive within a culture of innovation will agree: The collective genius is the company's greatest competitive advantage—indeed, its only one. Regardless of the industry, any innovation-driven organization without a staff of bright, bold, and energized employees quickly becomes tomorrow's roadkill. To staff and retain a workforce filled with intelligent, imaginative people is the best and only hope for survival as an innovation-driven culture.

One company in particular is famous for its quest for all-consuming brainpower. Microsoft hires for one thing: smarts! As founder Bill Gates says, "There is no way of getting around [the fact] that in terms of IQ, you've got to be very elitist in picking people who deserve to write software; 95 percent of the people shouldn't write complex software."[4] Microsoft's approach is straightforward: Hire the brightest people anywhere, pay them big bucks, and turn them loose. The software industry's general consensus is that great programmers are not just marginally better than good ones, but an order of magnitude better. The bottom line is that the one who hires at an order of magnitude above the norm wins. The main reason Microsoft keeps on winning is its collective craniums.

Another characteristic of a culture of innovation's unrelenting focus on brainpower is the economic downline effect. To take an example, it is observable that one superior programmer can create up to one hundred downline jobs, within the organization and the general economy. Through tapping the intellectual passion of just one superior programmer, countless opportunities arise. First, it becomes easier to attract other brain-rich talent to the company. Second, there is more likelihood of internal job creation for the company. Third come more opportunities for company growth into new products and services. Fourth, it increases the potential for job creation outside the company. A positive economic downline effect emerges.

CORE CULTURAL CONNECTIONS

There are several ways a culture of innovation connects with its employees.

A Need for Speed

Actor Tom Cruise, portraying a hot-shot navy pilot in his hit movie *Top Gun,* popularized what could be the mantra of all innovation-driven cultures: "I have a need for speed!" Speed to create, speed to market, and speed to upgrade are all critical to any successful innovation organization. Yet the frantic pace associated within most cultures of innovation is impelled not so much by management decree but by market mandate.

For innovative companies, the need for speed goes beyond product-development cycles and into the very core of operational success. The Home Shopping Network (HSN) of St. Petersburg, Florida, created the TV retailing revolution. Its internal computer systems are in the vanguard of sophistication, information analysis, and speed. On-air personalities view two monitors: One displays the signal being broadcast to all viewers, and the second displays an information screen filled with real-time data. HSN's powerful systems tabulate everything from the number of phone calls received, the number being answered, and the number of calls on hold to a perpetual update of sales data (number of units sold, number of units in inventory, total sales dollars). Such real-time data give every HSN on-air host the power to calculate the potential success of any on-camera item within two minutes of its appearance. If the item looks like a slow mover, another is quickly brought on-camera. HSN has transformed its need for speed into an amazing competitive tool.

Great employees connect to the need for speed within cultures of innovation. They love the opportunity to employ better and faster technologies to create and shape the future.

Cannibalization and Creative Destruction

Imagine working in an organization determined to create a new product that will eliminate the company's own top selling product line. For most organizations, this would be akin to eating its young. Yet when Lewis Platt, CEO of Hewlett-Packard, said, "We have to be willing to cannibalize what we're doing today in order to ensure our leadership in the future,"[5] he spoke directly to the core connection behind his company's continuing leadership in PC printers. As Platt and other leaders of innovation-driven cultures know, the willingness to cannibalize the company's successful products and services before the competition does must be an inherent connection between employees and the company.

Cannibalization and "creative destruction" reign supreme in most successful cultures of innovation. Regardless of what the organization's current bestseller is, it relentlessly pursues new, better, faster, and more powerful products or services. With the combination of knowledge half-life and the realization that market dominance can be measured in weeks rather than years, cultures of innovation must encourage cannibalization and creative destruction to remain competitive.

Employees of excellence find it an exhilarating challenge to take apart today's best to create tomorrow's winners. Top talent welcomes the opportunity to play with, tinker with, and simply smash existing processes and products in the search for new, better, faster, and even more fun ways to create the future.

Freedom to Succeed

An important corollary to cannibalization and creative destruction is the absolute mandate to give employees the freedom to succeed. World-class innovation and creativity never occur within organizations populated by overregulated, overmanaged, and overcontrolled employees. Successful cultures of innovation actively encourage employees to challenge the status quo in a never-ending quest to produce new and better products and services.

When living within a culture that promotes the freedom to succeed, one outcome is certain: Mistakes will be made. Many companies, whether innovation-driven or not, struggle and fail because of management's inability to tolerate mistakes. The attempt to create play-it-safe policies and procedures that significantly limit the chance of mistakes chokes the very nature of innovation.

Successful cultures of innovation are built upon management's active encouragement of a particular process of making mistakes: Make them quickly, make them at low cost, learn from them, and move on. Technology leader Hewlett-Packard is such a strong proponent of giving employees the freedom to succeed that one of its basic operational premises is "we reserve the right to make mistakes." HP knows, as do all other successful cultures of innovation, that to play it safe and limit mistakes is to remain hopelessly mediocre.

Top innovation-driven cultures emancipate action for their employees. Employee emancipation is defined as "giving people the protection they need to excel, the power to control their own destiny, and then getting out of the way."[6] To remain competitive, cultures of innovation continuously give employees wide latitude of experimentation as they strive to create the future.

Great employees within innovation-driven companies connect to an environment that allows the freedom to succeed. They flourish within organizations that offer the freedom to complete their work within broad operational boundaries. Without the freedom to succeed, employees are likely to seek new work opportunities where mistakes are encouraged and employee emancipation is guaranteed.

Take It to the Limit

As we noted in discussing Nordstrom in Chapter 3, the golden rule within many leading cultures of innovation is that there are no rules! As in NASA's Apollo moon missions, innovation-driven cultures push the edge of the envelope every day. Only by constantly stretching existing technology, processes, and systems to the limit can these cultures produce the quantum leaps in advances so necessary for organizational survival.

Mavericks abound within leading cultures of innovation. Their passion for taking all elements of their work to new heights helps their companies maintain an edge in development and delivery. Coupled with the ever-present battle to fight product obsolescence, the innovation-culture winners are those that allow their creative mavericks ample space to push, push further, and push even more, testing the very limits of every aspect of the operation. That is why such innovation leaders as Cisco Systems invest up to 11 percent of their annual budget in research and development. Without such huge investments, even today's networking giants would quickly become tomorrow's forgotten heroes.

Great employees relish taking their work to the limit. When not allowed to stretch the confines of their processes and push their equipment to the hilt, talented employees become bored and restless very fast. But with a living philosophy of taking it to the limit, innovation-driven winners remain a step ahead.

Have Fun: Kill the Enemy

Such is the mission of the phenomenally successful high-end software developer PeopleSoft. Fun is often a vital part of a culture of innovation. The incredible pressure to perform; the mandate to create faster, better, and more powerful products; and the endless push to outperform yesterday's successes all combine to create an often high-stress, high-pressure workplace.

The pursuit of fun is an emotional and psychological release. Witness the unheralded popularity of the *Dilbert* syndicated comic strip. Toiling away within a faceless, mundane, and oppressive workplace, *Dilbert*'s characters offer an in-your-face look at a humorless environment. The real fun of the *Dilbert* series is that such workplaces are everywhere. Yet such an environment is deadly for innovation-driven culture. When robbed of the natural need to laugh, lighten up, and have a little fun, workers succumb to the overwhelming pressures characteristic of a culture of innovation that quickly squelch all employee efforts in their quest to create the future.

Interestingly, an all-too-common companion of the fun factor in innovation-driven cultures is a passion to "kill the enemy." The enemies may be external competitors, both large and small. Sometimes the enemies are internal, such as complacency, departmental bloat, and missed deadlines. Regardless of where they reside, the enemies of a culture of innovation must be found and destroyed.

In combination with the previously discussed state of perpetual paranoia, "have fun: kill the enemy" resonates strongly with top employees. They unabashedly concur that only a take-no-prisoners approach can achieve market dominance. Employees love to win while having some fun along the way. They crave being in an atmosphere of innovation-driven companies that embraces this pairing of motivational goals.

The Thrill of Adventure

Intense, exciting, hectic, stressful, fast-paced, focused, casual: These are some of the words that employees we know use frequently to describe their innovation-driven culture. Such a combination of diverse emotions hardly affords employees a relaxed and easygoing work environment. On the contrary, a culture of innovation is one of the most stressful work environments in existence. Yet it does offer one guarantee that is sensuously appealing: the thrill of an adventure.

Lars Kolind, president of Oticon Holdings A/S, a leading Danish international hearing-aid manufacturer, says that a key to its success is "making people happy and secure while they are working in a very unstructured, chaotic, difficult, and ever-changing environment." Intel uses the phrase "Make a significant difference or get out of the way." Quantum, HP, and Apple all have similar philosophies. In each case, the mandate to be great, if nothing else, ensures a thrilling ride toward creating the future.

The thrill of adventure in innovation cultures is often accompanied by a payoff for success that can be just as gratifying. Particularly in the computer software industry, there is incredible excitement in watching a company's rising stock value or contemplating the worth of additional stock options. Few of us can discount the potential motivational appeal of a bulging stock portfolio in a growing, successful company. Yet financial gain, albeit exhilarating, is not always the primary thrill for employees.

For many employees within a culture of innovation, the greatest thrill is earning the right to join the next hot-project team. Once on that roller coaster, it is tough to get off. Even within an environment of killing hours, the adrenaline rush from project successes is often more appealing than any personal financial gain. Being part of today's (and potentially tomorrow's) hot-project teams is a significant motivator for many top employees.

Great employees within innovation-driven cultures connect to the thrill of the adventure. They realize that part of the high inherent in their career is the dizzying gamut of emotions they experience along the way. Intense pressure, unrealistic deadlines, and a breakneck pace all add to the excitement of the journey.

Cisco Systems: Making History Every Day

There are any number of things [hot buttons] we could tell you about Cisco [networking giant] in this space to entice you [subliminal messages] to explore a career here [bonuses, stock options], but what's the point? [you're unique] You've heard countless superlatives [best, best, best!] from all the companies; what could we possibly say [blah, blah, blah] to entice you into getting connected at Cisco Systems?

So opens the "Culture" page on Cisco's Website. Compelled to read on, you find in the next paragraph a magnificent yet subtle description of why Cisco will continue to dominate Internet networking through their employment mission, which is: "Connecting the right people to the right jobs, and superlatives won't work when we're talking about your career. You need real answers without the hype and genuine assistance in exploring whether Cisco is the right place for you."

Refreshingly candid. Technologically advanced. Progressively cool. Excitingly unique. These are the feelings that arise as you scan your computer screen—and all of this from merely surfing their Website. You might think the Cisco site is just another example of today's pervasive problem of overblown public-relations hype. You might think that Cisco is just another company painting a beautiful picture of what it is and what it stands for, without the organizational substance to back it up. If you think this about Cisco, think again!

Cisco Systems is the worldwide leader in networking systems for both the Internet and corporate intranets. Living the mission to "shape the future of global networking," Cisco's networking solutions "connect people, computing devices, and computer networks, allowing people to access of transfer information without regard to differences in time, place, or type of computer system."[7] Headquartered in San Jose, California, and with major operations in Research Triangle, North Carolina, and Chelmsford, Massachusetts, Cisco develops and sells networking products in more than ninety countries, with 13,000 employees worldwide. With FY 1997 sales of $6.4

billion, Cisco Systems holds the number one or two position in virtually every market segment it competes in.

Think Cisco; Get Connected

Cisco is built upon connections: people connecting to
each other, to the mission, and to the company. This connection starts at the top. President and CEO John Chambers is absolutely passionate about blending his
company's high-tech focus with a high-touch leadership
style. His unrelenting goal is to have his employees
"know my voice, my touch." Beyond the standard quarterly management meetings now commonplace in most
progressive companies, Chambers goes a step further to
connect with his employees by sponsoring a monthly
"birthday breakfast." Designed exclusively for frontline
employees, Chambers explicitly discourages executives
from attending, thereby encouraging an open (and often
brutal) communication forum. Employees quickly connect to the opportunity for directly interacting with their
leader, for challenging corporate goals, and for uncovering leadership gaps between top management and the
front line.[8]

Innovation-Driven Every Day

The Cisco culture is suffused with people and systems
focused on innovation. Although currently owning 75
percent market share in network routers and 40 percent
market share in network switches, Cisco is obsessed with
cannibalization of its products. The goal is to render its
products obsolete every six to twelve months. With the
radical pace of knowledge half-life, Cisco knows that to
maintain competitive advantage and to achieve its mis-

sion "to shape the future of global networking," it must sustain a culture that thrives on creative destruction of existing products.

Cisco's innovative spirit is also seen in many progressive corporate strategies. A major growth vehicle for any innovating company is acquisitions, not only to obtain the targeted company's products and processes but also to acquire its knowledge-rich employees. But the people side of Cisco's acquisition strategy is simple yet powerful: not to dislodge employees or families unless absolutely necessary. As the world's leader in computer networking systems, Cisco leverages its networking expertise to encourage newly acquired talent to telecommute as a desired alternative to relocation. Embracing such an innovative strategy lessens the trauma for the outside employee involved in an acquisition, demonstrates Cisco's cultural commitment to its employee's well-being, and minimizes the expense of family relocations.

Another innovative strategy within Cisco is its contrarian view of benchmarking. Cisco sees the process of benchmarking as allowing other companies to set the standards. Cisco prefers to set its own standards. The take-it-to-the-limit approach does not allow the company to wait around to benchmark its performance to other companies, whether inside or outside the industry. Rather, Cisco benchmarks against itself, constantly pushing its own world-class standards to ever-higher levels.

Transforming a Graceless Process

Beyond Cisco's innovative strategies in such areas as product cannibalization, acquisitions, and benchmarking, perhaps the most noted and acclaimed cutting-edge programs reside within staffing function. Using continuous research from current and prospective employees, Cisco has designed an entertaining and information-filled process to attract top talent—wherever it may be.

Engineers (as with any other talented group, for that manner) hate the traditional recruiting process. Beginning with the agony of trying to find the right words to put on a paper resume and ending with a used-car-sales approach of haggling over price (compensation), Cisco completely redesigned and innovated the traditional staffing process. To describe it with a phrase used internally, the goal was to transform a graceless process. There are several key components to this transformation.

Hire the Top 10 Percent That Fit the Culture

Cisco is dedicated to—even obsessed with—hiring the top 10 percent of talent that fit the Cisco culture. Many innovation companies only try to hire top talent, regardless of the fit with the company culture. This is where Cisco blows away most competitors. By ensuring a strong fit with the culture, Cisco's innovation-driven culture sets its sights on new levels of productivity and market dominance.

What defines the top 10 percent of talent that will fit into Cisco's culture? Through creating a "top employee profile," Cisco learned that the top 10 percent are fundamentally curious, are results-oriented, embrace change, and are multidisciplinary, with an intense desire to make a difference. They also learned a very valuable lesson: The top 10 percent are basically passive job seekers.

Cisco's challenge, as with many innovation-driven cultures, is to lure the passive job seeker in other companies away from current positions. Traditional recruiting focuses on active job seekers, those out of work, recently downsized, or currently scanning the classifieds for a new position. Cisco knows that the top 10 percent are seldom out of work, are rarely the first to go during downsizings, and are unlikely to read classified ads. How, then, to connect with the top 10 percent?

Through a series of top-talent profiles, focus groups, and interviews with current employees, Cisco's people researchers discovered where talented-passive job seekers hang out: in places like movies theaters, art fairs, microbrewery festivals, and home and garden shows. Cisco began placing advertising in movie theaters and became a more visible presence at the locations frequented by passive job seekers—including the *Dilbert* home page. Yes, Cisco has a hot link in that very place many top talents visit for a laugh. Perhaps most impressive and most innovative, however, are Cisco's own Website staffing efforts.

Website as Advertising Link

When you visit the Cisco home page and click on the "Jobs@Cisco" button, the first thing you see is a headline graphic that shouts: "We know where your friends are—Welcome to Cisco—Would you like a job?" Cisco leverages its Website not so much as a classified ad but more as an advertising link, trumpeting the power of the culture to lure top talent into applying with an industry leader. Choosing from a menu of offerings that range across hot jobs, benefits, university relations, diversity, and job fairs, Website visitors are enticed to click on the "culture" button. This is clearly a site that defines the Cisco corporate culture as an innovative one.

The culture page discusses Cisco's purpose, mission, communications strategies, flexible approach to work, diversity process, and work environment, as well as programs and facilities available to employees. This last listing boasts that Cisco's employees are some of the most well-known experts in networking, so why not work with the experts?

Such an innovative focus within staffing practices has paid a huge dividend for Cisco. More than 60 percent of all hires are referrals from current employees, a fact that significantly decreases the traditional costs of non-referral recruiting. More than 90 percent of all hires go through Profiler, an online application process, again reducing the cost of traditional paper-pushing recruiting and heightening the quality of the applications culled in the process.

Learn, Contribute, Grow

Keeping great talent at Cisco involves far more than the traditional activities of chanting slogans and waving banners. To begin, just scan the following list of services available to employees:

- ▼ Cafeteria (opens early, 7:00 A.M.; closes late, 7:00 P.M.)
- ▼ Onsite dry cleaning pickup and delivery
- ▼ Onsite stationery store
- ▼ Onsite car wash program
- ▼ ATM, stamp vending machines, mail room privileges
- ▼ Shuttle buses to CalTrain and rapid-transit stations
- ▼ Commuting vouchers
- ▼ Fitness center with professional staff and classes
- ▼ Volleyball and basketball courts, walking and jogging trails

▼ Multiple annual fairs (health, safety, earthquake preparedness, etc.)
▼ Internal e-mail aliases; special interests from gardening to technology

These benefits are the tip of the iceberg of efforts to retain top talent. Norman Snell, the director of global compensation, benefits, and HR operations, sees his role as focused on driving the Cisco culture through retention and rewards activities, rather than simply tinkering with compensation and bonus plans. Since he knows that culture fundamentally determines retention of excellent employees, he focuses much of his energy on a few potent cultural drivers.

First, everyone is an owner at Cisco. Every employee has opportunities to own company stock. As of mid-1998, 48 percent of the more than $2.5 billion in unvested gain at Cisco is held by individual employees, a huge number that powerfully demonstrates the employee-as-owner philosophy. In total, Cisco gives 4.75 percent of equity back to employees, a massive reinvestment to current employees.

Second, Cisco targets base pay at the 65th percentile, just above average. This is well in line with most other world-class companies, which pay comfortably above average without the desire to join the all-too-common high-stakes bidding wars. With a powerfully balanced retention program, like other aligned organizations Cisco has found you need not pay in the extreme to retain superior employees. It is far more important to create an exceptional culture that allows winners to hang around other winners.

Third, alongside his colleague Beau Parnell, the director of human resources and organizational development, Snell devotes significant time to reminding people of the larger mission of the company. Parnell notes that technical employees have a passion to "learn, grow, contribute, and have an impact on the industry." He also readily proclaims that "people love to go on a crusade," and seven of every ten employees at Cisco are "techies," possessing a passion for the latest technology toys. Consistent with the mission, Cisco reinvests 11 percent of its budget into research and development, further reinforcing its commitment to shape the future. The result of such retention processes is a single-digit turnover rate, an almost-unheard-of low number in a technology and innovation-driven culture.

The drive to fulfill the mission is at the heart of Cisco's culture of innovation. From technology to its growth and human-resource practices, Cisco is clearly a great example of such a culture. When asked by the authors why he stays at Cisco, Snell said it best: "Because we're making history every day!"

NOTES

1. Andrew S. Grove, *Only the Paranoid Survive: How to Exploit the Crises Points That Challenge Every Company and Career* (New York: Currency/Doubleday, 1996).
2. Interview with executives of Cisco Systems (May 4, 1998).
3. James Martin, *Cybercorp* (New York: AMACOM, 1996).
4. Randall E. Stross, *The Microsoft Way* (Reading, Mass.: Addison-Wesley, 1996), p. 35.
5. Alan Deutschman, "How H-P Continues to Grow and Grow," *Fortune* (May 2, 1994), pp. 90–94.
6. Jim Harris, *Getting Employees to Fall in Love With Your Company* (New York: AMACOM, 1996), p. 99.
7. Cisco Systems Website, "Cisco Fact Sheet" (March 1998).
8. Matt Goldberg, "Cisco's Most Important Meal of the Day," *Fast Company* (February–March 1998), p. 56.

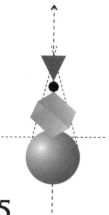

CHAPTER 5

A CULTURE OF OPERATIONAL EXCELLENCE

"It is unthinkable to hire, promote, or tolerate those who cannot or will not commit to this way of work."

—Jack Welch, CEO, General Electric

Jack Welch made this statement in his 1998 annual letter to shareholders and employees. His passionate commitment to "this way of work" leaps from the page. What is he so forcefully promoting? He is leading the charge to build at GE a corporate culture obsessed with operational excellence. But GE is not alone in its passion for operational excellence. The United States has witnessed phenomenal growth in the number of successful companies that embrace this culture, now including such house-hold names as McDonald's, Toyota, and Xerox.

The underlying purpose of an operationally excellent cul-ture is to create processes that minimize costs while maximizing productivity and efficiency. Such a process focus allows opera-tionally excellent companies to quickly recognize and contain unnecessary production and delivery costs that add little value. Although outsiders might call them cheap, operationally excel-lent companies are proud to be some of the world's most cost-conscious businesses. Yet as penny-wise as they are, operation-ally excellent companies seldom fall into the trap of being pound-foolish in their quest for world-class productivity.

> The underlying purpose of an operationally excellent
> culture is to create processes that minimize costs while
> maximizing productivity and efficiency.

Maximizing productivity and efficiency is critically impor-tant within operationally excellent companies. Attention, re-sources, and dollars are constantly invested in the tools necessary to increase productivity and decrease cycle time. Whether in manufacturing, retail, education, or services, these companies are obsessed with creating a lean, mean, smoothly operating machine.

Competitive advantage stems from process excellence in product or service creation and delivery. From seamless supplier chains to virtual inventories, operationally excellent companies strive to create systems that ultimately keep costs low while maintaining state-of-the-art production and distribution sys-tems that maximize economies of scale.

Although the other core-culture components of customer service, innovation, and employee spirit are important, the key emphasis within an operationally excellent culture is on process efficiencies. Through such emphasis on efficiency, these cultures attain the other standards of excellence too, as customer service and satisfaction rise, innovation flourishes, and employee satisfaction and job security increase.

> Through emphasis on process efficiency, operationally excellent cultures attain the other core standards of excellence too, as customer service and satisfaction rise, innovation flourishes, and employee satisfaction and job security increase.

A SIMPLE FOUNDATION

Although attaining process excellence can at times be extremely complicated, its foundation is quite simple and straightforward. Nucor Steel of Charlotte, North Carolina, a $3.6 billion specialty steelmaker, exemplifies this realization. A leader obsessed with operational excellence, Nucor's chairman Ken Iverson says, "Seventy percent of [our success] has to do with culture." How so? Nucor's strategy and culture is wonderfully simple: to build steel manufacturing facilities economically and to operate them efficiently. Nucor builds the same basic mini mill design throughout the country and then teaches employees to "simply produce more products for less money." Nucor's operationally excellent culture is the model for today's intensely competitive steel industry.[1]

General Electric is another example of a culture obsessed with operational excellence. Leaders abound within GE who encourage their 260,000 employees to become zealots for Six Sigma quality, the rigorous quality improvement program that focuses on reducing defects to 3.4 defects per million processes. For such a hugely diversified company as GE, this means 3.4 defects for every million aircraft engines, every million light bulbs, and every million appliances, locomotives, financial service transactions, or power systems produced and delivered.

McDonald's is another global enterprise with a culture of operational excellence. Whether in Moscow or Miami, a McDonald's hamburger is prepared to exactly the same standards of excellence. Springing from its four foundation beliefs (quality, service, convenience, and value), McDonald's "Hamburger Universities" (training facilities) are known worldwide for their emphasis on teaching the fundamentals of operational excellence to every franchise manager in every nation possessing a McDonald's restaurant. With such an obsession for process excellence, McDonald's is an inspirational model for worldwide success of any culture driven by operational excellence.

BIG PAYOFFS

Although an intense focus on operational excellence does not come cheap, the payoffs can be staggering. For example, GE invested over $450 million in 1998 in quality initiatives alone but expects that the effort will return more than $1.2 billion to revenues. L. L. Bean, the nation's largest outdoor catalog company, recently completed a $38 million, 650,000-square-foot order fulfillment center in Freeport, Maine, to better handle the company's business of more than $1 billion. The result: An order that five years ago took two weeks to fill and deliver can now be processed and packaged for overnight delivery within two hours.[2]

EFFICIENCY: OVERCOMING THE "HERBIES"

In his best-selling novel *The Goal*, Eli Goldratt offers an elegant example of another key to operational excellence: overcoming process bottlenecks. During a camping trip with his son's Boy Scout troop, the main character realizes that the scouts can only march as fast as the slowest marcher, a boy named Herbie. Everyone slows down or stops so Herbie can catch up. Herbie therefore becomes the bottleneck to the overall operational efficiency of the marching troop.[3]

Operationally excellent cultures relentlessly focus on eliminating the "Herbies," those sometimes recognizable and sometimes tough-to-find bottlenecks to productivity. Precise internal performance measuring and feedback systems revolve around specific work processes to better uncover many elusive Herbies. New streams of processes are then created to overcome, eliminate, or minimize the impact of such process roadblocks.

QUALITY STILL LIVES

Operationally excellent cultures often frame their process-improvement foundation principles upon the works of such familiar quality gurus as W. Edwards Deming, Joseph Juran, and Philip Crosby. Companies today blend the best ideas from such giants into their unique cultural needs, thereby creating their own special approach to process excellence. The overriding element common to these approaches, however, is an absolute focus on improving the processes that sustain their unique competitive advantage within their respective markets.

A significant aspect of operationally excellent cultures is their mandate for fact-based information. From change initiatives to new markets, information analysis is at the heart of process improvement. From fact-based assessments of market demographics, customer needs, and competitors, quality-driven organizations carefully study how to create, develop, and deliver their products to best meet strategic goals.

Cultures of operational excellence continue to embrace the

now-famous Japanese management concept of *kaizen*. The quest for permanent, daily, continuous improvement is of paramount importance. Without emphasis on personal and professional *kaizen*, the competitive advantage of operationally excellent cultures inevitably suffers.

CORE CULTURE CONNECTIONS

Here is how a culture of operational excellence connects to employees in several important ways.

Standardize

Although centralized planning as a political system may have died with Soviet communism, as an economic model central planning is alive and well. Operationally excellent cultures often go against the grain of current popular management thinking. Rather than promoting a bottom-up, decentralized approach, many operationally excellent cultures promote a top-down, centralized approach.

Standardization is central to the success of a culture of operational excellence. Clear, consistent procedures ensure the uniformity that this model of core culture holds as essential to excellence. Whether buying a McDonald's Big Mac or a Ford Escort, customers are assured that through the company's standardization of process, the hamburger or the car is the same in Berlin and Boston.

Although many workers may disdain such a big-brother environment, the exceptional employees within operationally excellent companies thrive on being asked to follow standard policies and procedures. They understand that for the company to succeed, they must follow well-crafted, performance-enhancing standards. Great employees within operational-excellence cultures do not see performance to exacting standards as over-bearing; rather, they take pride in knowing their adherence to and focus on meeting such standards increases organizational competitiveness, success, and ultimately their own job security.

Get It Right

J.B. Williford (Jim Harris's father-in-law) is a wonderful man. A military man by profession, his value system is that there is only one way to do anything: the right way. "Do it right and get it right the first time" is how he lives and works. (Naturally, as with many of us, the right way is usually his way.) He is absolutely passionate about doing things the right way. He beautifully connected to the military way and was a perfect fit for the air force's operationally excellent culture.

Getting it right means doing everything possible to make the process work the first time. Rework is a cardinal sin. Anything that impedes first-time pass-through quality is assessed and corrected. All efforts are geared to ensuring a first-time, every-time process.

Getting it right also means making the right tools and resources available to the right people so they can succeed. Imagine the car rental giant Hertz attempting its phenomenally successful and efficient check-in system (leave the plane; ride a bus directly to your car; get into the prestarted car; drive away) without the proper up-front informational process and tools. It's absurd to even consider an alternative approach, and that's the point. Yet many organizations attempt just that, undertaking similar get-it-right processes without having the right people, tools, and resources, and often failing miserably.

Great employees within operationally excellent cultures connect to the get-it-right approach to work. They have a passion for first-time quality. They take enormous pride in not only doing the right thing, but in doing it the right way—the company way.

Measure Twice, Cut Once

While running a custom home building company in the 1970s, I learned a valuable lesson that was told through an old carpenter's adage: Measure twice, cut once. All great carpenters carefully measure their wood cuts once, and then again, ensuring maximum accuracy and minimum error. As a result, fewer costly errors occurred when we took the time to double-check our measurements. Yet when errors did occur, whether in the measurement or the cut, I have often heard carpenters say, "Well, a carpenter can hide his mistakes—but a doctor buries his." There was another lesson in that bit of humor: Mistakes are vigorously avoided within operationally excellent cultures, but they are also understood within the grander scheme.

A more popular rendition of the measure-twice, cut-once connection is that "if you can't measure it, you can't manage it." In an operational-excellence culture, everything is measured. If it moves, if it does not move, or if it even thinks it might move, it is measured. Numbers are attached to literally everything, from the initial concept to the end product. Employees in operationally excellent cultures receive a sometimes overwhelming array of information, data, and process analysis upon which to measure and improve their performance. Whether by quality, quantity, time, or cost, such precise measurement allows the company to fine-tune every aspect of the process.

Top-notch employees in cultures of operational excellence connect to constant measurement of their performance. The measurement systems immediately give them feedback as to whether or not they are doing well or where they need to improve. Great employees applaud the real-time feedback systems available and are often self-motivated to improve their work without supervisor input.

"Stay Within the Lines; the Lines Are Our Friends"

A few years ago, a popular TV commercial portrayed a stately schoolteacher admonishing the class to "stay within the lines; the lines are our friends." The camera pans to one student who is daydreaming of smashing his 4 × 4 pickup truck through a large cake and defiantly driving quite outside the lines for an off-road mountain adventure. This student would have difficulty connecting with an operationally excellent culture.

Operational excellence mandates that employees stay within the lines of process excellence. Indeed, the (guide)lines are their friends. Individualism is not abolished within such a culture, but restraints on unlimited individuality are necessary to maintain order. Following carefully crafted, researched, and revised operation guidelines is the sure path to success. For example, the McDonald's operation manuals spell out in great detail what every employee needs to know to meet the company's rigid standards. Included within these manuals is everything from the obvious (the exact temperature for cooking their famous french fries) to the not-so-obvious (how each bathroom must be cleaned, and how often). Founder Ray Kroc achieved his dream of building a restaurant chain that would become famous for its uniformity of food preparation and presentation.

Rules reign supreme within cultures of operational excellence. Whether rules in procedures, process, or even product-line extensions, variety is rejected and procedures are king. Creativity and freedom of expression, although necessary for long-term excellence, are only allowed within well-defined parameters. For example, Tulsa-based Commercial Financial Services, the world's largest bad-debt collection company, has a three-volume procedures manual of incredible detail. According to credit card guru H. Spencer Nilson, such a rules-driven focus allows Commercial Financial Services to be "the largest, best-trained, and most efficient debt-collection operation in the world."[4] By staying within the lines at Commercial Finance Services, employees further their company's industry-leading performance.

Employees within such a culture understand the power of uniformity. They seldom view guidelines as constrictive but rather as guarantors that they are on the pathway to excellence. By staying within the lines, top employees maintain the momentum of operational excellence.

Waste Not, Want Not

In a culture of operational excellence, any waste is abhorrent. Precision in all endeavors is everything. Waste is spotted, attacked, and quickly destroyed. Throughout the 1980s, companies viciously fought against internal waste. A great example of superseding what was, just a few years ago, a horrendous waste of time, paper, and money is what is now a common commercial activity: the paperless intercompany transaction.

Virtual integration of producers, suppliers, distributors, and sellers has all but eliminated the paperwork of yesterday. Through electronic commerce and continuous-replenishment systems, tremendous waste has been eliminated; offenders have been forced into sometimes reluctant participants under the focus and insistence of operationally excellent cultures. For example, Wal-Mart's continuous replenishment system is unequaled in efficiency. Integration of product from factory to store is a marvel to behold; it's the company's key competitive advantage. Little effort is wasted in product ordering, and little effort is expended in moving product to the stores.

High-performing employees in cultures of operational excellence connect to the waste-not, want-not approach. They scour their work areas for undetected waste, enthusiastically sharing both their discoveries and remedies.

SmithKline Beecham: Simply Better

Simply Better (SIMPLY adv. + BETTER adj.). Phrase belonging to or associated with the company SmithKline Beecham. Denotes a way of working that encourages continual improvement by each individual. Simply = keeping things simple, efficient, and straightforward. Better = an inherent desire to continually improve, to gain an advantage.[5]

In 1989, the U.S. company SmithKline & French merged with U.K.–based Beecham to create what was at that time the fourth largest health care company in the world, SmithKline Beecham (SB). SB senior management understood from the outset the tremendous opportunity they had in the merger to create an entirely new culture founded on the rich history of both companies. To be a world-class company, they began the "simply better" journey, an ongoing strategic process that has transformed SB's combined culture into one of operational excellence.

Today, SB's pharmaceutical division produces and markets many of the world's top anti-infection, cardio-pulmonary, and vaccine products. Perhaps most known for their consumer health care division, SB also makes such household over-the-counter drugs as Contac, Tums, Aquafresh, and Nicoderm. SB is also a world leader in pharmaceutical benefits management services, clinical laboratory work, and in health care management and cost containment services. With 1997 sales of $12.7 billion, SB is a steadily growing giant in the global health care industry.

Process, Process, Process

The foundation for SB's culture is its S-D-C-A/P-D-C-A process. All process management at SB begins with a Standardize, Do, Check, Act (S-D-C-A) process that helps ensure consistent, reliable results. Once S-D-C-A creates the desired level of operational excellence, all related projects or activities then embrace the Plan, Do, Check, Act (P-D-C-A) sequence, SB's systematic process approach to working smarter.

Process thinking and process management are critical to SB's continuing success. Whether in health care services, pharmaceuticals, or benefits management, all employees strive to achieve efficient, effective, standardized, and reliable processes. Fact-based analysis is therefore essential, moving SB beyond reliance on intuition in all key business initiatives. Long-term business improvement initiatives are linked to daily work, thereby propelling continuous, incremental improvements toward corporate goals.

Measurement is another key ingredient to the success of SB. As CEO Jan Leschly likes to say, "If you're not keeping score, you're just practicing." Critical-step measurements enhance SB's ability to make real-time adjustments and improvements to overall processes. Although ultimate value is measured in the customer's eye, SB trains all employees on the value of the individual's work and how it adds to overall operational excellence.

Simply Better Staffing

As Dave Pernock, senior vice president of sales and marketing, points out, SB's innovative staffing processes are simply better because of their focus on being personal, consistent, and involved. SB relies on internal management, not external recruiters, for the majority of its staffing needs. Pernock believes that internal management gives a "personal, refreshing review of the company" to candidates, something no outsider can do. Further evidence of the power of the personal approach is that SB employee referrals account for more than 40 percent of all new hires. Armed with a brochure and audiotape titled "The Company You Keep," which describe the SB culture and workplace, employees actively recruit candidates through one-on-one personal contact.

A uniquely personal demonstration of the SB staffing process is the town hall recruiting trip. Teams of SB managers fly into medium and small-sized towns to share one-on-one about the SB culture and career opportunities. Most important, they treat the applicants as customers, sharing annual reports, giving overviews of current projects, and allowing candidates to ask any questions they like about working at SB. This progressive twist to the now-common corporate town hall meeting helps SB stay ahead of the competition in attracting top talent.

Perhaps the most novel personal staffing technique in SB's current arsenal is its simply-better process-improvement approach to campus recruiting. After seeking permission from the college, SB sends out managers to walk around the campus, talk to students about what they look for in a prospective employer, and ask how SB can become a better recruiter—and they ask the students to talk on tape! Not only does distributing the resultant taped comments throughout the SB system help improve campus recruiting processes; it sends a powerful message to the students that SB cares, listens, and is constantly focused on process improvement. Many students say they can't believe that a company actually sends someone to campus before the on-campus interviews to ask for their opinions and ideas.

Regardless of location, SB's recruiting process is rigorous, standardized, and consistent. All managers involved in the recruiting process attend internal training programs and are certified on the SB way of recruiting. Whether in Belfast or Brooklyn, internally trained recruiters can consistently apply their standard processes to uncover top talent. Further, with such a standardized staffing process, SB minimizes wasted time, reduces unnecessary duplication of effort, and streamlines its global staffing processes.

Simply Better Retention

SB's retention strategies are furthered by many outstanding processes, but none is more powerful than the focus on continuous learning, keeping employees in the loop, and communicating to employees the company's expectations of all its leaders. To jump-start productivity among new hires, SB complements individual testing with up to twelve weeks of rigorous product and services training. An annual recertification process promotes continuous learning for field staff. SB's Center for Strategic Leadership drives lower-level and midlevel management learning through an annual credit-based program. Managed by the Philadelphia College of Pharmacy, the program requires participants to read for and pass a certain number of mandatory and elective credits every year or face remedial training.

SB understands how keeping employees in the loop of company information is critical to high retention. During a recent potential merger, SB executives stayed connected to employees by using a toll-free phone number to call their "voice mail town hall." Key questions were taken from the voice mail and answered on a weekly internal broadcast to all company operations. Employees, nervous about the potential impact of the merger, were motivated to stay as they heard open, honest answers to expression of their concerns. Many divisions sponsor regular "meet the boss" symposiums where employees in groups of fifteen to twenty are allowed to ask any question they wish, including anonymous queries written on note cards.

Leadership behavior is a key element in SB's retention success. Managers are rewarded and promoted based upon their ability to drive the core culture. Furthermore, employees are told what they can expect from their leaders, including being involved in challenging and meaningful work, supported in their attempts to improve process, recognized and rewarded for their contributions, given honest and open feedback on their performance, and treated as a true team member through honest and fair interactions. Through such a focus on leadership behaviors and employee expectations, SB connects with its high-performing employees, which results in enviable levels of retention and productivity.

Fostered by the vision of top management, designed around the foundation of improving core processes, supported by new-thinking, staffing, and retention programs, and encouraged through management's showing that it has the courage to walk the leadership talk, SmithKline Beecham's "simply better" way is a great blueprint for operational excellence.

NOTES

1. Kenneth Iverson, *Plain Talk: Lessons From a Business Maverick* (New York: John Wiley & Sons, 1997).

2. Kate Kane, "L.L. Bean Delivers the Goods," *Fast Company* (August-September 1997), pp. 104–113.

3. Eliyahu M. Goldratt, *The Goal* (Croton-on-Hudson, N.Y.: North River Press, 1992).

4. Jerry Useem, "The Richest Man You've Never Heard Of," *Inc.* (September 1997), pp. 43–59.

5. Excerpted from the handbook "Get Involved—It's the Way We Win," outlining SmithKline Beecham's corporate approach to cultural renewal.

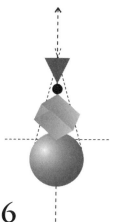

CHAPTER 6

A CULTURE OF SPIRIT

"If you take care of your people,
they'll take care of you.
If you don't take care of your people,
they'll take care of you."

Years ago, while attending an executive training program, I (Jim Harris) heard these lines from a workshop leader. This simple but forceful message burned into my consciousness and also made its way into my notes at the seminar. The presenter's powerful message is a fine example of the primary philosophy of the newest emerging core culture in corporate America and elsewhere: the culture of spirit.

The culture of spirit is quickly gaining ground as a recognizable and primary core culture. From seeds planted in the 1980s, spirit-driven cultures have grown to become one of today's mainstream business realities. From such pioneering companies as ServiceMaster, Chick-fil-A, AES Corporation, and

Tom's of Maine emerged a new business model, one that is not afraid to tap into the human side of business.

Executives in spirit-driven cultures do not fall into the trap of touting that "employees are our company's greatest asset." Rather, they proclaim that employees *are* the company, and they back it up with a sincere, concerted effort to build a culture that uplifts the spirit and energizes the soul. The assumption is simple: By taking care of its people, the people take care of the business. Process, customers, and innovation are important, of course, but no more so than tapping the spirit of the individual employee.

Spirit-driven companies are obsessed with creating environments that unleash the limitless creativity, enthusiasm, and energy of people. They often embrace a higher calling, a special cause, or a unique path to personal enrichment, all to better themselves and the world. Whatever can be done to shape the work environment to better enable an employee's natural gifts, values, and abilities to emerge is a top priority. Competitive advantage is therefore gained not so much through machines and process, but rather through the collective energy and spirit of employees bound together by a special cause.

WHY SPIRIT—AND WHY NOW?

There are many reasons why spirit-driven cultures are the fastest emerging core corporate culture in the United States.

Backlash to Downsizing

The first is the backlash to proliferating and continuing corporate downsizings. Downsizings by their very nature imply a lack of concern for employees. However unfair this implication may be, frontline employees equate downsizing with *bad*. Radical competition, globalization, and, yes, poor management have all had a negative impact once perceived as a permanent connection between employees and employers. Many of today's excellent employees are looking for a connection that surpasses yesterday's broken promise of job security.

Pay Inequity

A second reason for the fast growth in spirit-driven cultures is the huge discrepancy between frontline and CEO pay. It seems we read every day of another CEO receiving a massive stock payoff even as the company cuts staff, closes facilities, and misses operational plans. Such massive inequity eats at the very heart of employees, diminishing their already tenuous loyalty to the company and creating a chasm of disbelief between the front line and the executive suite. Although employees realize they have little control over how much pay their company executives receive, they cry for rational (and even emotional) explanations as to why they should recommit to their companies. Many of today's great employees are looking for connections to their companies that bridge the abyss of pay discrepancy.

Declining Prospects for Advancement

Third, the narrowing career advancement ladder is producing a distinct shift to more spirit-driven cultures. With layers of management disappearing daily, so goes opportunities for promotion and advancement. Because many employees today continue to be motivated by advancement opportunity, they become frustrated as the obvious next career steps disappear. Great employees are looking for company connection beyond promotions.

Workplace as Social Community

The fourth reason for the growth in spirit-driven cultures is that the workplace has become the new social community. Not too many years ago, the primary social community was the neighborhood where we lived. We all vividly remember the neighborhood where we grew up. Perhaps we knew everyone who lived on the block and for the several blocks around us. We even knew all the neighborhood dogs by name, their owners, and which ones would bite! Yet today's average employee is working longer hours than ever before, and spending more time with work colleagues than with families or neighbors. The company has become the social community. Deep and lasting friendships are now more likely to emerge among workmates than among neighbors. Employees are even more likely today to know the names of their coworkers' pets than their neighbors' names! Spirit-driven companies recognize the reality that today's employees are looking for a deeper social connection to the workplace and fellow coworkers.

Employee Disillusionment

The fifth reason for the growth in spirit-driven cultures is the overall disillusionment of many of today's workers. Most employees today do not want to feel stuck in an organization or job for which they feel no passion, no great calling. They want to feel fulfilled, to enhance their lives and the lives of others. Many disillusioned workers (notably former military officers) are now looking to nonprofit organizations for personal fulfillment.[1] Spirit-driven cultures often connect with employees in deeply personal, fulfilling ways.

THREE TYPES OF SPIRIT-DRIVEN CULTURE

Spirit-driven cultures tend to fall within three broad categories: religion-focused, socially focused, and employee-focused.

Religion-Focused Cultures

Perhaps the most controversial emerging culture on the corporate landscape is the religion-focused culture. Their bold point of departure is an open and forthright belief in God, from which they grow the business accordingly. Sometimes condemned or even mocked for attempting to mix the seemingly irreconcilable realms of religion and business, these organizations stand firm in their belief that running a business on religious principles inspires employee excellence that in turn engenders productivity and profits.

Chiseled into a huge marble wall outside their Downers Grove, Illinois, headquarters are ServiceMaster's four objectives:

**To honor God in we all we do,
to help people develop,
to pursue excellence,
and to grow profitably.**

William Pollard helped grow ServiceMaster, a building cleaning and maintenance giant, into a multibillion-dollar service business guided by religious principles. The culture builds employee dignity through a focus on the "soul or spiritual side of the person doing the task."[2] Going against popular opinion, Pollard contends that "God and business do mix. For us, the common link between God and profit is people."[3]

S. Truett Cathy took a similar approach in building Chick-fil-A, a closely held fast-food company headquartered in Atlanta. The corporate purpose at Chick-fil-A is (1) to glorify God by being a faithful steward of all that is entrusted to us, and (2) to have a positive influence on all who come in contact with Chick-fil-A. According to Cathy, being a success in business is the best way to honor his religious beliefs. The results are impressive. Even with a six-day workweek (stores are closed on

Sunday), Chick-fil-A consistently outsells competitors that are open seven days a week and averages a less than 6 percent annual store management turnover versus a 40 percent industry average.

Hundreds of spirit-driven companies across America are more open and obvious than ever before about how they build their cultures upon religious principles. For example, the mission at Silver Dollar City in Branson, Missouri, the successful amusement park management company, is to "create memories worth repeating in a manner consistent with Christian values." Interstate Battery, based in Dallas, provides employees with opportunities for religious study, growth, and outreach. Leaders at Hall-Mark Electronics, an electronics distributor also headquartered in Dallas, often pray together on key business issues. These organizations suggest how diverse, religion-focused cultures do manage to blend their often-conservative yet time-honored principles into a profitable, successful enterprise.

Socially Focused Cultures

Until the 1990s, the thought of creating social change while earning profits was laughable. The prevailing sentiment was that social concerns were social concerns, business concerns were business concerns, and one could not mix the two. Not until progressive, socially conscious companies like Ben & Jerry's Homemade and Tom's of Maine demonstrated that social conscientiousness and profits were possible did corporate America begin to take serious notice.

Pragmatic idealism may best describe the approach of socially focused cultures. They are pragmatic in that they aggressively pursue business success, yet idealistic in that they possess a passion for having a positive impact on society. Motivated by this pragmatic idealism, socially focused cultures strive to unleash their employees' need to better themselves and the world around them.

Ben & Jerry's Homemade has traditionally measured success in terms of both profits and social issues. The Vermont-based specialty ice cream and dessert maker has weathered the sometimes scalding business commentary that accompanies any higher-road company that occasionally slips or falls into tough times. Yet cofounder Ben Cohen continues to fervently believe that "business has a responsibility to give back to the community." Accordingly, more than 7.5 percent of the company's pretax profits continue to be donated to worthy causes around the world. The Ben & Jerry's Foundation sponsors such socially focused programs as an all-children's Afro-Latin percussion band that fights drug abuse and homelessness; a project that provides farm animals to impoverished communities; and various housing and economic development programs. In addition to the pretax profits used by the foundation, one-half of the income generated through fees from visitors' plant tours is donated to specific community service groups in Vermont.

Even within its current move to tighten business practices under a new CEO (Perry Odak), Ben & Jerry's continues to stand firm in its support of social causes. Through Odak's infusion of more pragmatic business practices, the bottom line is improving, and with it the ability to support the social agenda they hold so dear.[4] With a renewed focus, Ben & Jerry's continues to be a wonderful work-in-progress on how to build and sustain a socially based culture.

Kinko's, the successful business services company, takes a slightly different approach to being a socially focused culture. According to founder Paul Orfalea, "our coworkers believe that they are contributing to something larger than Kinko's."[5] The Kinko's experience is more than just a business connection for the customers, a place for copying, report generating, bookbinding, and related office services. Rather, Kinko's is a primary social connection for customers—a place for independent, typically home-based businesspeople to gather, socialize, gab, trade horror stories, and help each other learn to run their businesses better. The entire in-store experience at Kinko's produces strong social connections among employees and customers, which in turn builds strong business connections.

From international missions of service to creating social connections for customers, socially focused cultures have emerged as a viable business model. Such trailblazers as Ben & Jerry's and Kinko's illustrate both the potential challenge and the rewards of taking a higher social road.

Employee-Focused Cultures

Employee-focused cultures walk the talk of placing the employee's needs at the forefront of the operation. Their uniqueness is based upon a simple premise: The best way to take care of business is to first take care of the people. In this way (and similarly to the way in which the employer can meet employees' religious or spiritual needs and their desire to be of service to social needs), as the company meets the needs of the employee, the employee is then better able to meet the needs of the business.

> As the company meets the needs of the employee (which can be said to include religious or spiritual needs and the desire to be of service to a social needs), the employee is then better able to meet the needs of the business.

Realize, however, that employee-focused cultures are not country club environments where employees are endlessly pampered. Actually, most employee-focused cultures are incredibly demanding operations with high standards of excellence (and corresponding expectations). Why is this the case? Thanks to their concerted efforts to take care of the employees' needs first, employee-focused cultures are able to ask for and receive enthusiastic employee performance.

Rosenbluth International, the Philadelphia-based multibillion-dollar travel company, epitomizes an employee-focused culture. CEO Hal Rosenbluth believes that "the highest achievable level of service comes from the heart, so the company that reaches its people's hearts will provide the very best service."[6] His company reaches its associates' hearts in a variety of ways. Their annual three-day company celebration for all 4,500 associates is called Live the Spirit. All headquarters meetings are posted, and any associate interested in the topic may attend. The "associate for a day" program lets employees shadow a senior executive for the day and learn firsthand how the company operates. Rosenbluth's best-selling book, *The Customer Comes Second*, further illustrates his focus on employees.

Although replete with the latest technology, Rosenbluth International sees it as merely a tool for the employees and not the focus of competitive advantage. Putting employees first is its chosen means to success. Rosenbluth's phenomenal success boils down to one powerful concept: to serve clients best, we have to put people first.

Employee-focused companies also include "family friendly" workplaces. Recently ranked the most family-friendly company in America by *BusinessWeek*, First Tennessee Bank is also one of *Forbes*'s financially top-performing banks for the past five years. According to First Tennessee spokespersons, the amazing array of family-friendly policies heightens employee commitment, which in turn produces outstanding service and profits.

First Tennessee's commitment to a family-friendly environment is more than just corporatespeak. It is spelled out in everything from employee handbooks to management training programs. Management understands that often the most powerful employee connection to the company is through the immediate supervisor. So First Tennessee trains and holds supervisors accountable for supporting their family-friendly programs.

CORE CULTURE CONNECTIONS

Whether religious, social, or employee-focused, a spirit-driven culture connects to employees in several important ways.

Servant Leadership

Servant leadership is the concept that the greatest leaders are first of all servants to those they lead. By serving her people first, the servant leader better understands the needs of the employee, can more quickly react to his needs, and can more easily coordinate the tools and resources necessary for his superior performance. Management decisions, policies, and even corporate direction all feel a positive impact through servant leadership.

A special bond is created in spirit-driven companies between servant leaders and the frontline people. They see management as caring, employee-focused leaders. This caring is reciprocated with strong bonds of loyalty and commitment to company goals. Although no more powerful than the bonds created within cultures built upon excellence in quality, service, or innovation, those within the spirit-driven culture center upon the humanness of work. A self-fulfilling prophecy emerges as the servant leaders focus on the human spirit of the workers, and in turn the workers reciprocate their spirit by striving toward organizational goals.

Another element of the servant-leader connection is its power as a role model for serving the front line first. When promotion-seeking employees within a spirit-driven culture encounter a servant-leader approach, they inherently duplicate this style within their own leadership activities. In effect, servant leadership helps extend to all levels a take-care-of-the-front-line-first management philosophy.

Work for a Greater Good

A powerful connection within spirit-driven companies is the common urge to work for a greater good. Whether focused socially, through religion, or on employees, connection to the common cause inspires excellence throughout the operation. Working for a greater good also taps into a subsurface human need: to leave a lasting legacy.

Incredible levels of commitment, sacrifice, and noble efforts can be observed within organizations dedicated to leaving a legacy. Whether we are willing to admit it or not, we all desire to do something for posterity. We all want to be remembered for something that stretches beyond our everyday existence. Many professionals give their lifetime of work to nonprofit organizations in order to do so. Religious institutions are a prime example. Thousands of other nonprofit groups exist not so much on the basis of cash flow as on the united flow of employee efforts to leave a legacy for those they choose to serve.

Private-sector companies can also attain the same level of commitment and connection as nonprofit organizations do, through helping employees develop a sense of legacy in their worklife. With sincere, honest, nonmanipulative effort on the part of senior management to work for the greater good, employees are far more likely to be self-motivated to contribute their piece of the legacy, be it an internal company project or one extending out to the community.

Build People First

Spirit-driven companies hold dear the precept that you must first build the person before you can ask the person to excel.

Spencer Hays, CEO of Southwestern/Great American Company in Nashville, a $600 million diversified publishing, clothing, and insurance company, says "You can't build a *business*; you build *people*."[7] At Timberland, the New Hampshire–based footwear manufacturer, they proudly state, "We are investors: We invest in employees." This build-people-first philosophy becomes a powerful connection between employees and the company.

A central tenet within most spirit-driven companies is an obsession to train, develop, and nurture all employees, regardless of level. It is easy and quite typical in corporate America to concentrate most employee development on management or highly technical jobs. In a spirit-driven company, this approach with its inadvertent neglect of the personal and professional growth needs of any group of employees is just short of blasphemous. Because an individual's dignity is held sacred within a spirit-driven company, building people first means building all people and not just the select few.

Faith, Hope, and Charity

The book of Hebrews (11:1) says, "Faith is being sure of what you hope for and certain of what you do not see." Spirit-driven cultures are known for their ability to connect hoped-for yet unseen results with the employee's desire to make a difference. This special connection of faith, hope, and charity is often the key to distinguishing a spirit-driven culture from the rest.

Whether through powerful missions, visions, celebrations, posters, or daily reminders, spirit-driven companies consistently reinforce to employees that they hold a joint journey along a different road from that taken by most workers. Employees are often overwhelmed with communications and information on their progress toward the united purpose. Although often considered too touchy-feely for quality, service, and innovation core cultures, spirit-driven cultures leverage the unique combinations of faith, hope, and charity to actively engage the hearts and souls of their workers.

Beyond the Bottom Line

Spirit-driven companies measure their success by a different set of standards from those of most nonaligned companies. Instead of measuring organizational success exclusively upon the bottom line, spirit-driven organizations tend to measure success and impact on more than just profit.

The standards by which spirit-driven companies measure success are as varied as the companies themselves:

▼ AES Corporation, a progressive power generating company headquartered in Arlington, Virginia, annually reports to stockholders its progress (or lack of it) in meeting their goals in terms of the values of integrity, fairness, fun, and social responsibility.

▼ The Noel Group, a Stevens Point, Wisconsin, travel business, publishes a booklet entitled "Foundations" that shares the foundation values and principles that cofounders John and Patty Noel embrace in their dedication to "leave a lasting legacy in life to make the world a better place for all of us to live." All proceeds from sales of the two-dollar booklets are donated to Noel Group's Make a Mark humanitarian program, dedicated to building orphanages, schools, and clinics worldwide.

▼ Patagonia, a leading outdoor clothing company, measures its success in environmentally friendly production. An open letter to customers in the 1997 fall catalogue lamented that "the production of our clothing takes a significant toll on our earth," and went on to profess the company's rededication to lessening such an impact.

Regardless of the path, spirit-driven companies often inspire long-term employee retention though measuring both company and individual success beyond the bottom line.

Competitive Yet Humane

Please do not be fooled: Spirit-driven companies are not weak, soft, cuddly places to work (Southwest Airlines is a good illustration in dispelling that notion). Their standards are just as high as those of other core cultures, and sometimes higher. Yet within pursuit of these high standards, they strive to maintain the humanness of business.

Some of the fiercest, most competitive business executives in America lead spirit-driven cultures. They often have an incredible desire to win, but not at all costs. Anything that could have an adverse impact on the special connection with employees is carefully evaluated. If forced to implement policies or programs that might negatively affect the special bond, spirit-driven companies quickly communicate the decision, discussing the ramifications and the rationale, and clearly communicating management's understanding of the impact. Spirit-driven companies keep the human connection even in tough times.

Spirit-driven companies also attempt to connect to the whole person. Rather than focus solely on the pocketbook or the operations manual, they find ways to consistently remind themselves that people are more than just a pair of hands and a pair of eyes.

Many progressive companies such as Eli Lilly in Indianapolis take a holistic approach to employee relations. Their policies and programs are designed to address the whole human being. Such a competitive yet humane approach is symbolic of spirit-driven companies in general.

VanCity Credit Union: Right Values and Good Business

Nestled within the magnificent Canadian Rocky Mountains, Vancouver is a progressive, shining-star city, the pride of British Columbia. There is a special spirit that inhabits the city of Vancouver, a spirit based on pride, purpose, and people. Befitting this spirit is a shining-star company headquartered downtown, one that epitomizes the pride, purpose, and people of this great city.

VanCity Credit Union is Canada's largest credit union. With total assets of $5.5 billion and 1,500 employees at forty-five branches, VanCity serves virtually every part of British Columbia. In addition to its core credit union operations, VanCity's subsidiaries include insurance services, a real estate development group, Canada's first branchless online bank, an investment management service, and a community foundation that supports charitable organizations in employment development, nonprofit enterprise, and affordable housing.

The basic business philosophy at VanCity is "We do good when we're doing good—we do good when we're not." Always striving to earn great returns for its members, VanCity is first and foremost a spirit-driven culture, an organization passionately devoted to supporting dozens of community-building programs throughout British Columbia. From the top down, employees are inspired to join in contributing to worthwhile projects that promote the greater good of both members (customers) and citizens. Here is just a sampling of the amazing array of social programs supported by VanCity:

▼ Loans to entrepreneurs based upon their character and credit history, not their collateral

▼ Business planning and funding for existing women's enterprises
▼ A community car-sharing network
▼ A food and community garden cooperative
▼ Environmental protection projects
▼ A recycling depot in downtown Vancouver
▼ Housing grants for women leaving prison
▼ Low-income housing projects
▼ Job skill development, education, counseling, and referral programs for street-involved youth

VanCity's most recent employee survey verifies the community commitment. More than 95 percent of employees believe that VanCity is a "valuable and contributing member of our community" and "encourages staff to be involved in our community." More than 87 percent would recommend VanCity as a "good place to work." This community-centered spirit is at the very heart of the credit union's success.

Corporate Image as Recruiting Magnet

Most companies fail to use the power of their community image as a recruiting tool. Not true at VanCity, which leverages its unwavering commitment to corporate social responsibility as the primary recruiting tool. External communications focus on corporate citizenry and the core values of social responsibility. Programs and policies center on how workers can best serve their members and their communities. VanCity's strategic community service image pays a huge dividend in its recruiting efforts.

VanCity's community image is based upon its corporate attitude to be seen as cooperative, flexible, helpful, socially conscious, resilient, and service-minded. This image, justified through the many community programs it supports, magnetically attracts like-minded citizens. They see VanCity living up to the rhetoric and are therefore attracted to apply. A larger group of citizens continuously applies for membership in huge numbers, based upon the organization's unique perspective.

The customer experience at VanCity is so powerful that members themselves frequently apply for jobs. As one manager described it, members "hunt us down, join us, experience us as a customer, love what they see, and then decide to want to work for us."

With such a spirit-driven corporate image, VanCity finds itself in the enviable position of often having too many superlative applicants from which to choose. VanCity's staffing and management approach is to "interview hard, manage easy." A competency-based interviewing system combined with multiple interviews is the preferred selection method. The combination of attracting through corporate image and interviewing through competencies allows VanCity the luxury of hiring the very best people whose values match its spirit-driven culture.

Keeping the Spirit Alive

Lauren St. John's role in managing her department of corporate spirit is to create opportunities ensuring that the special VanCity spirit remains alive within each employee. With the philosophy that "good morale is good business," her staff focuses on a variety of initiatives to keep top employees productive, happy, and loyal.

Employees are kept in the loop of company information through a variety of internal communication systems. Task forces and focus groups allow input into compensation and flexible benefits programs. Employee opinion surveys audit the culture and form improvement initiatives for the executive action plan team. CEO and executive breakfast programs allow employees face-to-face feedback from leaders on key business issues. Staff newsletters and electronic bulletin boards keep employees in touch with the latest corporate news.

Recognition and motivation programs at VanCity extend beyond monetary rewards into employee community involvement and personal development. The annual recognition banquet celebrates company success as well as reinforcing the behaviors important to team success.

Quality of life and employee training are critical to employees at VanCity's. With 89 percent women employees, VanCity invests significant time and resources in top offerings in employee well-being programs, child-care assistance, and flexible benefits. Programs that include job sharing, resource libraries, and life-skills programs all support the lifelong learning of VanCity employees. All together, VanCity maintains one of the highest employee retention rates in its industry.

With absolute dedication to the greater good, unrelenting passion to be held to a high standard, and ceaseless concern for improving the world around it (not to mention having a department of corporate spirit), VanCity Credit Union is a great example of a spirit-driven culture. The last sentence in the opening letter of the 1997 annual report beautifully summarizes the organization's corporate spirit: "For every time our members choose VanCity, it's proof that the right values and good business can succeed."

Little wonder that VanCity is the shining-star company of Vancouver.

NOTES

1. Hal Lancaster, "Disillusioned Workers Look to Nonprofit Organizations," *The Wall Street Journal* (April 13, 1998).
2. C. William Pollard, *The Soul of the Firm* (New York: HarperBusiness, 1996), p. 20.
3. Ibid., p. 22.
4. Paul C. Judge, "It's Not Easy Being Green," *BusinessWeek* (November 24, 1997), pp. 180–182.
5. *Fast Company* (January 1998), p. 166.
6. Hal Rosenbluth, *The Customer Comes Second* (New York: William Morrow, 1992), p. 24.
7. William Barrett, "An American Original," *Forbes Online* (December 1997).

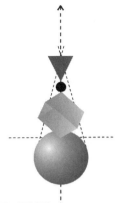

PART THREE

FINDING GREAT EMPLOYEES

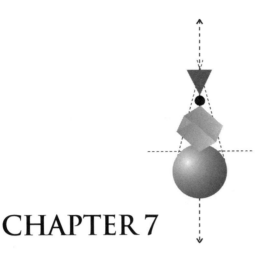

CHAPTER 7

BEST PRACTICES IN STAFFING

Staffing involves everything that an organization does as part of hiring an applicant. Staffing consists of two basic sets of activities: attracting candidates (employee recruitment) and screening candidates (employee selection). Specific activities include such things as:

- ▼ Defining job and organizational requirements
- ▼ Posting position openings internally
- ▼ Advertising job openings externally
- ▼ Evaluating job candidates
- ▼ Making the hiring decision

Organizations that staff most effectively link their staffing strategies to their corporate culture. We refer to these companies as *aligned*, and they are rare. Aligned organizations know their core purpose, and they incorporate it into everything they do related to staffing.

Aligned organizations (those effectively linking staffing strategies to corporate culture) know their core purpose, and they incorporate it into *everything* they do related to staffing.

EIGHT BEST PRACTICES IN STAFFING

We identify eight staffing best practices that aligned companies use to find great employees. These best practices work for two major reasons. First, they introduce the notions of job fit and culture fit into the staffing equation. Second, by incorporating the culture-fit component into staffing best practices, the employer creates strong cultural connections with the applicant before they are even hired. The company is therefore assured of hiring someone who can do the job and support the company's core culture.

Staffing Best Practice One: The "WOW" Factor

Tom Peters defines *WOW* as "stepping out (individuals at all levels in a firm and independent contractors) and standing out (corporations and other organizations) from the growing crowds of look-alikes."[1] The notion of the WOW factor has a significant impact on the effectiveness of staffing because it immediately sets aligned organizations apart from other companies. Not being seen as part of the crowd is a tremendous competitive advantage as a business recruits and selects applicants.

Aligned companies know what makes them unique relative to their competition. They also know how to communicate their uniqueness effectively to a well-defined target market. Most important, aligned organizations leverage their uniqueness to create a solid foundation for building a world-class workforce in which everyone supports the company's core cultural driver, be it customer service, innovation, operational excellence, or spirit.

Aligned companies "brand" their staffing process. Because they have a clear idea of what sets them apart, compared to non-aligned companies they are better able to communicate this important information to others. They incorporate their culture into all communications and activities related to the staffing process. They also place essentially equal importance on the two notions of job fit and culture fit. Given a choice, they look for applicants who fit well with the organization on both counts. This strategy perpetuates their culture and keeps them unique and successful relative to other companies.

Staffing Best Practice Two: Applicant as Customer

Nonaligned companies typically see applicants and customers as two separate and unique groups of people. Even when recruiting customers for jobs within the company, nonaligned companies tend to view their advertising, customer service, marketing, and recruiting activities as unrelated to one another.

Aligned companies, on the other hand, understand the value of treating the applicant as a customer, which they do in three ways.

Know What You Want in an Applicant

First, aligned companies know the qualities and characteristics of their ideal applicant just as well as they know the qualities and characteristics of their customer. It is not unusual for non-aligned companies to invest significant resources so as to know and understand customers. Nonaligned companies, however, rarely invest the same level of resources in knowing and understanding their ideal applicant. Many companies typically define the applicant as whoever responds to the classified ad or whoever completes an application.

Aligned companies invest considerable money, people, and time resources in understanding who the ideal applicant is, where to find this person, and how to make it easy for the ideal candidate to find and contact the company. Aligned companies then use this information to design unique and highly effective staffing programs.

Communicate the Same Message to Applicants and Customers

A second way that aligned companies treat their applicants as customers is by communicating a consistent, culturally aligned message to both customers and applicants. D. Wendal Attig, a nationally recognized expert in the area of corporate branding and founder of the Advisory Team in Clearwater, Florida, believes that "effective company branding requires a congruency between the promise that the company makes to customers and the promise that the company makes to its employees."[2] According to Attig, the promises made to the customer through advertising, marketing, and corporate branding significantly affect an applicant's ability to understand the company's core culture. In turn, applicants then judge how they might fit within that culture. It is therefore imperative to create branding messages consistent with the core culture so as to attract culturally aligned, potentially great employees.

Give Applicants a Positive Experience

A third way aligned companies treat applicants as customers is to ensure that all applicants have a positive staffing experience. Aligned companies go to great lengths to maintain an upbeat, positive relationship with all applicants—even those not hired. From friendly, personal contact with first-time applicants to carefully crafted rejection methods, aligned companies passionately focus on treating candidates so well that they quickly reapply for future openings (as well as remain lifetime customers).

Staffing Best Practice Three: Image Is Everything

Aligned companies create excitement and enthusiasm about their organization. This excitement makes people interested in working for the organization. The first step in creating excitement is to create a strong and positive company presence. Nonaligned companies often believe they have that already by virtue of constantly advertising for applicants. Job seekers may certainly be aware of the organization, but they may infer negative messages about the company if all they see are never-ending classified ads for openings within the company.

Aligned companies, on the other hand, create an image that portrays them as both community leaders and industry experts. Applicants form impressions about companies from various sources:

▼ The company's support of various local and civic organizations and causes
▼ The company's support of nationwide initiatives and programs geared toward social change
▼ The company's reputation in its industry, as described in industry-related publications
▼ The company's reputation as an employer, as described by past and current employees

The community and national causes supported by a company communicate a great deal about the values of the organization. The more your company is "out there" both in terms of being a successful business and in giving back to the community, the more likely it is that truly great applicants having a passion for the company's core culture will apply for a job.

Simply providing a general overview of your company in a classified ad, at a job fair, or on your Website is not enough. Aligned companies not only take advantage of opportunities but also create their own opportunities to get the word out about the company and its core focus. They do this by supporting local and national programs that are consistent with the company's core culture. Aligned companies have also been known to play up different aspects of their culture depending on the specific interests of the applicant or group of applicants they want to hire. This strategy does not mean that the company presents a different culture to different applicants. It does mean that the company emphasizes different aspects of its culture that it thinks would be most appealing to a particular applicant or group of applicants.

In a recent message on an Internet site for human resource professionals,[3] Mr. John DePolo, Vice President for Consulting for Bay Cities Research, Inc., in Palm Beach, Florida, described factors that affect people's decisions to change jobs. The factors included such things as interesting work, employer flexibility, a perception that employees can make a difference, and an apolitical environment within the company. Mr. DePolo suggested that even if all those factors exist, "it's vital that the community, at large, knows it. If you can, send your employees out into the technical community—to conferences, user groups, etc.—and make sure others know that it's a great place to work!"

This strategy is not only important to high-tech organizations; others can benefit from it as well. Creating a strong, positive, public image of your organization as a great place to work is critical to finding and keeping great employees. Yours can be the greatest organization to work for, but if only a few people know about it, you still have difficulty finding good employees. A very effective, yet often overlooked, strategy for finding great employees is to create and sustain a strong, positive, and very public image.

Staffing Best Practice Four: Get Real

Organizations, just like people, are strong in some areas and weak in others. Some organizations communicate their strengths and weaknesses openly in the early stages of the staffing process, while others do not. Nonaligned companies routinely use a best-foot-forward or first-date strategy with applicants because they do not want to risk losing them. What they do not realize is that they may keep this person in the short term, but they are likely to lose him in the long run. Putting your best foot forward results in wasted time and resources because applicants do not fully realize what they are getting into, and when they do, they may select out of the process. In nonaligned companies, applicants often do so only after they have been with the company for a while and experienced firsthand the strengths and weaknesses of the organization.

Aligned organizations, by contrast, know precisely where they are strong and where they are not. Moreover, they clearly communicate that information to all prospective new hires. Aligned companies see the value of "getting real" with their job candidates. They share "the good, the bad, and the ugly" early on in the staffing process. This does not mean hanging out dirty laundry in the initial interview, or describing in recruiting materials the downside of working for them. Aligned companies simply relate the positives and negatives of the job and the organization in an objective, nonevaluative manner and let the candidate decide whether this is an opportunity that she wants to pursue.

In the short run, candidates who are turned off by this dose of reality opt out of the staffing process early on. In the long run, getting real maximizes the fit between candidate and organization. The candidate knows much better what she is getting into because the organization has clearly communicated that information from day one.

Joseph Rosse and Robert Levin describe several examples of giving realistic previews, which is one way to get real with job candidates.[4] Examples include allowing retail candidates to observe or experience the work required between Thanksgiving and Christmas prior to hiring for the Christmas rush. Rosse and Levin also discuss one organization that makes a well-known consumer product with a fun image. This company makes the extra effort to give candidates tours of the factory floor and the offices so candidates know they are not "coming to work in Santa's workshop." If these examples sound impractical because of the time involved, consider a popular alternative: videotaping this type of experience. At a minimum, make sure you devote some time to discussing the pros and cons of the job and the organization in the interview process. Overall, this practice ensures maximum fit between the applicant, the job, and the organization.

Staffing Best Practice Five: Job or No Job

Aligned companies know that it is no easy feat to attract and hire top talent, especially those that are innately aligned with the core culture of the organization. In today's competitive labor market, good applicants do not remain applicants for very long. Companies must seize the opportunity when they find culturally aligned top talent.

Nonaligned companies typically use job openings to begin (and end) their job searches. A position becomes vacant and the company begins the staffing process for that position. The process stops when the position is filled. In nonaligned organizations, the job opening drives the staffing process. The nonaligned company's entire focus is on filling the job, and filling it fast.

Aligned companies do not wait for a job opening to occur before setting out to attract and hire culturally aligned talent. They keep their eyes and ears open constantly for good candidates. When they find them (and they always do), they hire them regardless of whether there is a specific job opening or not. They know top talent when they see it, and they create a place for it.

Staffing Best Practice Six: Multiplicity

Nonaligned organizations tend to stick to a small number of familiar methods to recruit and select employees. They run a classified ad in Sunday's paper to recruit applicants, and they screen job candidates through phone or one-on-one interviews. Moreover, when filling a position, they typically involve only one department or function in the staffing process. They have HR perform all the functions related to staffing, or they involve only the department that has the open position in the staffing process.

Aligned companies understand the value of using multiple methods and involving multiple people and departments in staffing their organizations. They run classified ads. They post their openings on their Website. They participate in job fairs. They sponsor community-related activities and provide employment information at those activities. They interview candidates. They test applicants. They do all of these things, and more.

Not only do aligned companies use multiple methods, but they also involve employees from various parts of the organization in the staffing process. If there is an opening in marketing, aligned organizations are likely to schedule a job candidate to talk with HR, the prospective supervisor in marketing, some of the coworkers in the department, and in some cases even internal or external customers of the position. Staffing is not just a human resource function in these organizations; it involves everyone in the company because the company views recruitment and retention as a major factor that is responsible for growing the business.

Staffing Best Practice Seven: The Great-Employee Profile

As previously noted, nonaligned companies tend to use job fit as their primary means of defining a great employee. They define the knowledge, skills, and abilities required in the job and then look at the match with the skills that the job candidate possesses. Nonaligned organizations do not usually think much about organizational fit; if they do, they tend to focus on very general, socially desirable applicant qualities such as being a self-starter or a good team player.

Aligned companies know who their ideal applicant is (see best practice number two); they also know precisely who their ideal employee is. Knowing the characteristics of the ideal employee further ensures that the aligned company maximizes the fit between the person, the job, and the organization. Precisely defining your ideal employee creates the standard by which you compare all applicants. This information is critical in creating, sustaining, or reenergizing a culture that supports your organization's core focus.

Aligned organizations often create a "great-employee profile" to help them sustain their cultural focus. The profile includes information about job requirements and expectations as well as personal characteristics that are associated with the company's culture. For example, someone who does not value serving others and solving others' problems is unlikely to remain in a customer-service organization. Someone who does not value cutting-edge thinking and creative solutions to problems is unlikely to remain in an innovation-driven culture. By incorporating information on organizational culture into your great-employee profile, you know better the type of person you are looking for and are more likely to keep that person after he is hired.

Staffing Best Practice Eight: Beyond Benchmarking

Nonaligned companies tend to use tried-and-true staffing methods, and once they are in place they rarely change. "We've always done it this way" underlies the nonaligned company's approach to staffing. External forces, such as a competitive labor market, drive the decision to change methods. If an external event occurs, nonaligned companies tend to react by looking to their competitors for ideas on how to improve their staffing process.

A final best practice separates aligned companies from nonaligned ones. The former do not wait for something to happen to force them to change their staffing practices. When these organizations find that a staffing practice is working for them, they do not become complacent and keep using that same method forever. They constantly challenge themselves and their employees to identify even better ways to find great people.

A related characteristic that aligned companies share is that they do not copy what other companies are doing. In fact, other organizations usually copy them. Just as significant personal growth comes from introspection or looking inward, significant business change and growth often comes from looking inward. Aligned companies involve employees at all levels in answering the tough questions surrounding how staffing practices can best support the company's vision, purpose, and future direction. Even though aligned companies investigate and consider what other companies do related to staffing, they typically do not weigh that information too heavily. They also do not need that information to move forward in making changes in their own programs.

Going beyond benchmarking suggests that there are two ways aligned companies differ from the nonaligned. First, aligned companies know the status quo; they track and measure organizational performance frequently. From a staffing standpoint, they collect and analyze metrics related to the staffing function so they know, at any given moment, what is working and what is not. The metrics consist of more than simply calculating cost-per-hire, or monthly or annual turnover rates for different positions or locations within the company. Aligned companies measure the relative frequency of use of different recruiting sources, the average time to fill a position, and, moreover, the quality of employees hired using their staffing methods.

Second, aligned companies know there is always room for improvement. No matter how good things might be, aligned companies know that things can be better. They constantly strive to make things better.

> To have a fully aligned staffing function, you must measure what you currently do and use that information to revise and improve. Measurement is the key for keeping and improving staffing practices that consistently attract culturally aligned top talent.

To have a fully aligned staffing function, you must measure what you currently do and use that information to revise and improve. This information provides the foundation for determining what works and what does not and allows adjustments to be made as needed. Measurement is the key for keeping and improving staffing practices that consistently attract culturally aligned top talent.

NOTES

1. Tom Peters, *The Pursuit of WOW* (New York: Vintage Original, 1994), p. xi.

2. D. Wendal Attig, personal communication (April 28, 1998).

3. John DePolo, "High Tech Recruiting Practices," HRNET@ cornell.edu (April 17, 1998).

4. Joseph Rosse and Robert Levin, *High-Impact Hiring: A Comprehensive Guide to Performance-Based Hiring* (San Francisco: Jossey-Bass, 1997).

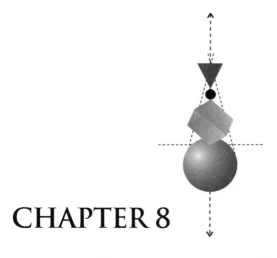

CHAPTER 8

STAFFING BEST PRACTICES IN ACTION

Aligned companies lead the pack in the quality of applicants they recruit and select. Contrary to popular opinion, aligned companies possess no magic formula or secret weapon for successful staffing. They use the same tools that are available to everyone else. They hold job fairs, they advertise and post their job openings, they interview job candidates, and they test job prospects. They do all the things that go along with finding good people. The big difference between aligned companies and their nonaligned counterparts lies not in what they do but *how* they do it.

PUTTING WHAT'S BEST INTO ACTION

Regardless of the core culture, aligned companies integrate most, if not all, eight best-practice strategies described in Chapter 7 into their staffing function. This chapter provides dozens of examples of how they do it. Since one of the goals of this book is to help you create an action plan to better align your staffing strategies to your core culture, please strongly consider the following advice. As you read the many examples within each best practice in this chapter, ask yourself the following questions:

1. How do you currently integrate the eight best-practice strategies into your staffing function?
2. How might you integrate the essence of each example into your current staffing plan?
3. What needs to be modified, expanded, eliminated, or created to integrate these examples into your existing staffing programs?

Through answering these questions, you jump-start your action plan preparation and are much closer to aligning your staffing strategies to your core culture.

Staffing Best Practice One in Action: The WOW Factor

As we saw in the previous chapter, the WOW factor refers to how companies capitalize on their uniqueness to create an environment that applicants want to work in. Aligned companies use the WOW factor in their staffing practices to communicate their uniqueness in all that they do prior to hiring a candidate. Here are some great examples of how various companies incorporate the WOW factor into their staffing processes.

▼ Girls (and Boys) Just Want to Have Fun.

Southwest Airlines provides one of the best examples of how a spirit-driven culture can incorporate the WOW factor into its staffing function. Southwest capitalizes on a reputation as being a fun place to work and reflects that reputation in its classified advertising as well as hiring practices. For example, one recruiting ad shows a teacher scolding a little boy. The tag line of the ad reads, "Brian shows an early aptitude for working at Southwest Airlines . . . at Southwest Airlines, you get check pluses for breaking the mold. For 'coloring outside the lines.' " Another ad shows a photograph of CEO Herb Kelleher dressed as Elvis. In the ad, the tag line reads, "Work in a place where Elvis has been spotted. Send your resume Attention Elvis."[1]

Southwest goes even further to ensure that the culture of fun is reflected in its hiring process as well. Through a variety of group-hiring activities, the company assesses applicants and hires employees who are other-oriented, outgoing, and have the same sense of fun on which the company culture was built.

▼ Get Personal.

Winchester Hospital, in Winchester, Massachusetts, provides a wonderful example of how any innovation-driven culture can use the WOW factor effectively in its staffing practices. The hospital profiled Michael Gogola, the new chief information officer, in its recruitment efforts to take the facility in a new direction regarding information technology. According to Gogola, "We wanted to attract the best and brightest people, and we wanted something that would differentiate us from the endless array of technical openings listed in the newspapers."[2] So, the ads displayed a photograph of Gogola and described his efforts to update the hospital's technology. Other efforts to personalize recruitment efforts at Winchester included providing onsite child care facilities and offering free ski lift tickets during the winter for employees who submitted referrals of qualified individuals for possible recruitment.

▼ There's No Place Like Home.

In a strategy that could be effectively used in any customer-service culture to increase stronger customer connections, the city of Dubuque, Iowa, used the WOW factor to fill the city's labor shortage. Dubuque launched a "come home" campaign, with city leaders focusing their recruiting efforts on former residents. They figured, *Who is more likely to appreciate the city's culture and be willing to move to Dubuque than a former Dubuquer?* The city began the campaign during the holiday season to take advantage of former residents' visiting relatives in Dubuque, hoping that the relatives too would play a key role in persuading their visitors to consider moving back to Dubuque.

The leaders of the recruiting effort also put 28,000 inserts into alumni magazines from Iowa universities, and they even sent letters to graduates. The city has also launched a come-home Website that lists local job openings and allows job hunters to apply for jobs online. The site also lets returnees shop electronically for houses and cars—and reminds them where to get a fishing license.

▼ When Are You Leaving?

Lockheed Martin, known for its culture of innovation, offers a unique benefit to employees that many see as an effective and unusual staffing tool to lure employees who will support Lockheed's innovative culture. An entrepreneurial leave of absence program allows employees who want to start their own business to do so, using two years of unpaid leave and having to pay only the company's rate for health insurance during this time. Once the two years is up, the employee can either leave the company or return. Lockheed Martin benefits in two ways. First, the program is relatively unique and therefore a strong recruiting tool. Second, for the successful employee spin-off ventures, the company makes equity investments and strikes licensing agreements.

▼ Cool Places.

Federal Express provides a great example of how an operationally excellent culture can incorporate the WOW factor into staffing. FedEx recruiters noticed that it took a long time to find and hire information systems (IS) workers with the right mix of technical skills. One reason was that many young professionals did not want to relocate to the company's corporate headquarters in Memphis, Tennessee. Rather than trying to force applicants to see the benefit of living in Memphis, FedEx moved many of its new IS positions to Dallas, Colorado Springs, and Orlando. Talented IS recruits now have their choice of locations. This strategy proved to be very attractive and thus good for the company in terms of finding and keeping employees who support their culture.

Staffing Best Practice Two in Action: Applicant as Customer

Companies that treat their applicants as customers know their applicants as well as, or even better than, they know their customers. They also ensure that each applicant has a positive experience with the company during the hiring process. Regardless of whether the applicant is hired or not, the company gains or maintains a valued customer. Here are some good examples of how various companies treat their applicants as customers.

▼ **Casting a Net.**

Cisco Systems, known for its innovation-driven culture, uses Profiler, an online resume creator of the company's own design, to allow the applicant to "paint a picture of yourself that differentiates you from everyone else." Profiler's easy-to-fill-in boxes allow Cisco to carefully analyze each applicant's core motivations and skills, evaluating them so as to quickly identify a good potential match.

Another good illustration of Cisco's innovative culture and customer-service approach to dealing with applicants can be found in a sidebar with Profiler. Since applications generally arrive during regular business hours of 10:00 A.M. to 3:00 P.M., while most applicants are at work, Cisco provided an "Oh no, my boss is coming!" hot button. Realizing that a supervisor or colleague might step into the applicant's work area while the employee is filling out an application to go to work for Cisco, the hot button automatically puts up a screen that displays a bulleted list of "Seven Habits of a Successful Employee"! The list includes such success habits as taking risks, embracing change, not settling for just an OK project or job, and demanding innovation. Two more lists are also accessible: a "List of Gift Ideas for My Boss and Workmates" and "Things to Do Today," which includes getting your Halloween costume from the dry cleaners. If this is not enough to communicate to the Website visitor during the application process what the culture is like at Cisco, at the end of the Profiler application is a line that says, "OK, the fun's over—get back to work!"

▼ **Radical Rejections.**

Ben & Jerry's Homemade provides one of the most striking examples of how a spirit-driven culture treats its applicants as customers. Several years ago, it announced a "Yo, We Want You to Be Our CEO" contest. Advertisements in most of the nationally known business publications prompted 20,000 ice cream fanatics to apply for the position. Author Harris applied but was sadly shocked that he was not called in for an interview. He was, however, even more flabbergasted at what he received in response to his query.

Enclosed in his "rejection" packet was a full-size Official Rejection Letter—suitable for framing. The multicolored certificate had a picture of Ben Cohen and Jerry Greenfield, side by side, each wearing a huge top hat emblazoned with the logo of his favorite Ben & Jerry's flavor (White Russian and Chocolate Chip Cookie, respectively). With the caption, "We almost wanted you, Jim Harris, to be our CEO," it went on to say that "it warms our hearts—and blows our minds—that someone of your high caliber would even consider a career with us. Your talents and potential convinced us that a much higher calling awaits you. You're just too valuable to the world to be peddling ice cream. Be happy, go lucky."

Also included in his "rejection" packet was a coupon for a free pint of Ben & Jerry's ice cream as well as a Call for Kids brochure that discussed several worthwhile children's agencies located in Vermont, with encouragement to contact local agencies to volunteer.

▼ Trolling the Aisles.

Organizations with an innovation-driven culture could learn a thing or two from Amy Naples, a technical recruiter for Bluestone Software in Mount Laurel, New Jersey. Visiting a local bookstore, she noticed a group of young men browsing through books on Java and C + + programming in the computer section of the store. Like any successful recruiter, she immediately strolled over and started talking about openings at her company and handing out business cards. She says, "It's just become part of my life. There is not a technical person I meet who I do not ask whether they know of another high-level technical person looking for a job."[3] (Naples admitted taking her recruiting efforts one step further by putting her business card in books that she thinks her best prospects are likely to read.)

▼ Cop a Coaster.

Sanchez Computer Associates, in Malverne, Pennsylvania, uses a great staffing strategy that any customer-service–driven culture could use to strengthen its culture: recruiting the customers of other businesses. Sanchez is a banking services software company that encourages job candidates who visit Flanigan's Boat House, a restaurant in a nearby technology-oriented corporate center, to "steal this coaster, and win a free lunch" by taking along a bar coaster that advertises jobs at Sanchez. Flanigan's customers are primarily young people who work at the corporate center; qualified candidates who bring a coaster to an interview at Sanchez receive a certificate for a free meal at the restaurant.

▼ **Location, Location, Location.**

Some customer-service–driven companies treat their applicants as customers by playing up their location in recruiting efforts. Liberty Mutual Information Systems, located in Portsmouth, New Hampshire, is ninety minutes northeast of Boston. Liberty Mutual recently emphasized its location in radio ads by mentioning easy access to numerous ski resorts and outdoor attractions on the coast. Since it competes with Boston's many high-tech companies for top talent, the company emphasizes what offers that the applicant is likely to find appealing and can only get by working there.

Staffing Best Practice Three in Action: Image Is Everything

Creating a strong, positive image in the marketplace is a defining characteristic of aligned companies that successfully incorporate the culture into staffing practices. Here are some good examples of how various companies create and leverage the company's image to effectively find and hire great employees.

▼ **Go Back to School.**

Capital Holding, located in Louisville, Kentucky, is one of the largest stockholder-owned life insurance companies in the United States. It is a wonderful example of how an operationally excellent culture can create a strong, positive image in the marketplace. Over a three-year period, Capital Holding committed more than $3 million to learning-related programs. Former vice president John Franco initially realized the need for a well-educated workforce for the 1990s and beyond. The company, the Jefferson County school system, and Pleasure Ridge Park High School agreed to develop a curriculum that would begin to meet the needs of the business, the community, and the students.

The result was Project Business. Today, it is one of the best of the more than 140,000 school-business partnerships in the United States. The program provides Capital Holding with a direct link to intelligent, dedicated students who have business skills and work experience. It gives high-achieving, bright students from blue-collar neighborhoods an opportunity to develop work skills and to consider attending college.

Twenty students are selected for the program. To be chosen, students must have a good grade point average, analytical ability, good attendance, and typing and communication skills. The program also requires that instructors recommend students for the program. Each year, one Pleasure Ridge Park High School student is awarded a four-year scholarship to a local college of his or her choice. The student must maintain at least a 3.0 GPA as a full-time student, have teacher and employer recommendations, and maintain employment part-time at Capital Holding.

▼ **Take a Stand.**

Ben & Jerry's surfaces yet again as another example of how a spirit-driven culture can create an image that communicates its spirit to customers and potential employees alike. The first time Ben & Jerry's ever considered taking a public stand on a government policy involved their Peace Pops program. Ben Cohen recommended that the company get involved in One Percent for Peace, an organization that supported redirecting one percent of the military budget to peace through activities intended to support peaceful efforts.

Initially, Ben faced serious opposition—especially when he proposed renaming their ice cream bars as "Peace Pops" and printing a message supporting One Percent for Peace on the wrapper. Management felt that this action would turn off customers, ultimately resulting in products being pulled from the stores and putting their employees out of work. Some managers felt that it was not right to take a stand against the government, and they did not want the company to support such activity.

The board of directors decided to support the program. The

Peace Pops effort created Ben & Jerry's reputation for "social activism," a reputation that continues to this day. Through their efforts to effect social change, Ben & Jerry's leverage their image as a social change agent to attract applicants who share the values of this unique and successful company.

▼ **The Dodgers Way.**

The Los Angeles Dodgers educates its employees regarding the history of the organization and, by doing so, strengthens its commitment and connection to customers. The Dodgers create and sustain their winning image through various staffing-related activities. For example, as soon as a player arrives at rookie camp in Vero Beach, Florida, he begins to learn about the roots of the organization. They show a film of history of the organization—starting back in 1890. During spring training, three nights a week, the players must report for discussions. The Dodgers bring in guest speakers to talk about how to plan for life after baseball and what it is to have pride in the Dodgers tradition.

The recruits learn, from day one, the "Dodgers Way" of doing things. The Dodgers Way is not just about playing baseball. It's about how people are treated, and that comes from the top of the organization. This means the owners, the O'Malley family, and what has been passed on all these years will continue to be passed on.

Obviously, the Dodgers Way works. In a very competitive and high-turnover business, the Dodgers have had tremendous continuity and stability. Since 1954, the team has had only three managers, four general managers, three farm directors, and three scouting directors. People love working for an organization with a winning image, and it shows.

▼ **Work and Learn.**

Le Vieux Manoir au Lac, a hotel located in Murten-Meyriez, Switzerland, prides itself on its customer-service culture. The hotel's enthusiastic, friendly, and professional staff is a key constituent of its culture. It is no accident that the hotel directors, Erich and Elisabeth Thomas, have hired consistently great employees. The Thomases are active in the community, and they use community involvement to their advantage in finding employees who share their commitment to customer service.

For example, they participate at local fairs in Murten, a nearby town, where they and their staff write skits and perform with accompanying music. The Thomases also developed an intern study program for students from the hotel school in Lucerne. They also encourage cross-training programs for their staff at other restaurants and hotels; one of their young maître d's spent time at Auberge du Soleil in Napa Valley.

▼ **Hot Buttons and Beemers.**

Walt McGhee, eastern regional director of Xerox Corporation's new channels division, knows how to create an image. The mission of his division is to challenge Hewlett-Packard's dominance of the network laser printer market. Organizations with an operationally excellent culture could learn a lot from him. He once met an applicant who was an avid motorcycle fan and owner by driving to the interview on his own BMW motorcycle.

Another way that McGhee creates an attractive company image is to capitalize on the weaknesses of a candidate's current company to get him to come to work for Xerox. For example, a candidate sent him a resume that said he worked at "MicroAge (a $4 billion master reseller organization)." McGhee flew the candidate in from Boston and they met at McGhee's country club in Riverside, Connecticut. Over dinner on the back porch, which overlooks Long Island Sound, McGhee asked, "Why would you be interested in a long-term career with a company that requires an explanation?" Although the applicant initially turned down the employment offer, McGhee did not take no for an answer, and he finally did hire him.[4]

Staffing Best Practice Four in Action: Get Real

Aligned companies get real with their applicants so that both the company and the potential employee know what they are getting into and can make an informed decision about employment. Companies that present themselves to applicants honestly and in a balanced way save time—both the applicant's and the company's. More important, getting real creates strong cultural connections and maximizes the fit between the person, the job, and, ultimately, the company. Here are some examples of how various companies are up front with their applicants during the staffing process.

▼ **Seeing Is Believing.**

Eckerd Corporation, a retail drugstore chain headquartered in Largo, Florida, employs 76,000 people. To assist store managers in hiring hourly employees who will support the organization's customer-service core culture, the company provides a hiring kit. Among other things, it includes a video for the store manager to show to all hourly applicants prior to interviewing them.

Often, applicants assume that the job is only what they see employees doing when they visit the store. The video is intended to better align applicants' expectations in terms of what the job really involves and requires. The Eckerd video stresses the importance of employee attitude ("We want people who like to work with people, and people who are willing to go out of their way to help people"). It shows real-life situations with customers where the employee has to do more than just stand behind the counter and ring up the sale. In the video, employees perform some of the behind-the-scenes aspects of the job: unloading trucks, stocking merchandise, helping customers find merchandise, and cleaning bathrooms. It also presents an overview of all the departments in the store (cosmetics, express photo, front-end, and pharmacy) where hourly employees work.

Feedback on the video from store managers has been very positive. According to John Kucmierz, HR staffing and systems manager, applicants typically have more questions about the job after watching the video. Also, he noted that in some cases the video successfully helps applicants select themselves out of the hiring process. As a result, store managers do not waste their time interviewing applicants who are not seriously interested in the job in such a customer-service culture.

▼ $100 to Ride.

Applewood Plumbing, a customer-service organization located in Denver, pays its applicants for the privilege of getting real. As part of the hiring process, the company pays $100 to any applicant who expresses interest in a service technician position with their company. There is only one catch: The applicant must ride and go on service calls with a current service technician. The applicant benefits by getting a dose of reality about the job. The service technician, who is specially trained on how to evaluate applicants, provides valuable information to the company about how well the applicant relates to the job and to the customers.

▼ You've Got to Have Friends.

The title of the classic Bette Midler song "You've Got to Have Friends" is a fine description of an innovative and incredibly successful activity that drives cultural connections at Cisco Systems. To help would-be applicants better understand the Cisco culture, they are matched with a "friend" inside the company, someone in the same area of work interest and with similar career goals. This connection allows the current employee to offer candid, straight answers to the applicant's many questions on the challenges, culture, opportunities, and frustrations of working at Cisco. The friends program is designed to last well into the applicant's first few weeks of work, if hired. This unconventional mentoring approach builds strong connections throughout the Cisco system and jump-starts new-hire productivity.

▼ **Engineer Your Career.**

Texas Instruments, the Dallas-based computer products company, uses a tool that assesses candidates both professionally and personally for cultural fit in an operationally excellent culture. The tool was developed by Personnel Decisions, an international HR consulting firm in Minneapolis, as a kit entitled "Engineer Your Career." It contains a disk that opens up into a brochure describing Texas Instruments—its products, history, and values.

Following the introduction is a self-selection tool that asks candidates to respond to thirty-two questions about work preferences, such as work environment, working conditions, and relationships. For instance, one question asks how the candidate feels about smoking in the office; possible responses range from strongly agree to strongly disagree. At the end of this section, the computer displays a bar-like graph that indicates the candidate's compatibility with the company. If a potential problem exists, the tool so informs the candidate. In the case of smoking in the office, if the applicant responded that he or she felt strongly in favor of smoking, the computer would signal that the company has a nonsmoking environment. The tool also highlights strong matches. This insider's view allows applicants to make an informed choice prior to considering an offer.

▼ **Watch Them Work.**

In a factory in Greer, South Carolina, BMW built a simulated assembly line to assess candidates' ability to perform jobs within an operationally excellent culture. As part of the hiring process, job candidates have ninety minutes to perform a variety of work-related tasks. Charles Austin, a consultant with Development Dimensions International of Pittsburgh, helped design the facility. He suggests that people who do not have the mental energy to meet BMW's requirements do not get hired. This example demonstrates effective use of job simulations, which are probably the ultimate way for companies to get real with their applicants.

Staffing Best Practice Five in Action: Job or No Job

Aligned companies know the value of finding culturally compatible top talent. In fact, these companies often hire outstanding job candidates even if they do not have a specific job for them at the time they are hired. Here are some examples of how various companies incorporate a "job or no job" philosophy into staffing practices.

▼ **Immune System.**
Dave Bolles, director of the staffing resource center at 3M, described a practice that clearly demonstrates 3M's commitment to hiring top talent in support of its innovation-driven culture. The "designated requisition process" is a method by which 3M approves hiring someone before the actual job is available.

Each year 3M projects its hiring needs, and the company authorizes a percentage of those hires before actual jobs are posted. This process allows 3M to make offers to their very best candidates regardless of whether they have a specific opening or not.

To further demonstrate 3M's commitment to the job-or-no-job philosophy, all designated requisitions are immune to cancellation. That is, the company guarantees that all designated-requisition positions are funded. This action recognizes the need to bring in new talent and keeps the company from cutting funding for campus-level recruiting activities and programs. This action also guarantees ties with college recruiting programs even during times of slow or weak financial performance within the company.

▼ Hire for Culture, Train the Job.

Raymond James Financial, a financial services company headquartered in St. Petersburg, Florida, uses a staffing strategy that any operationally excellent culture could use to find people who support such a culture. Raymond James has lived the job-or-no-job philosophy since the business began thirty-five years ago. At that time, the company knew that the local talent pool of people with financial service experience was limited, at best. Management figured that if they hired bright people who fit the culture, they could train them on their specific job.

According to Gena Cox, vice president of assessment and employment, the philosophy continues to this day. According to Cox, "If you hire bright people who fit the culture, you can train just about anything else." She says that finding bright people who fit the culture is more difficult today because of the low unemployment rate as well as increased competition for financial-service industry talent.

One recent example where Raymond James Financial demonstrated its commitment to the philosophy involved someone who applied for a compensation analyst position. In reviewing her skills, managers found out that this person had significant experience in compensation as well as experience in human resource information systems. Instead of hiring her for the analyst position that was posted, the company created a new position, vice president of compensation and HRIS, that would benefit the company and maximize her skills once hired.

▼ When Opportunity Knocks.

To best support a spirit-driven culture, Ben Cohen and Jerry Greenfield believe that a values-led company needs to take advantage of the opportunity, whenever it arises, to hire highly qualified people who are aligned with the company's values.

Hiring people who have been schooled for ten or twenty years in the traditional way of doing business, they say, can be a real negative. They also claim that when they hire from the outside, they are hiring an unknown quantity. Many times, people hired from the outside do not work out. The pair found that when the company promotes from within, they know what they are getting. Cohen and Greenfield have tried it both ways. They hired people for their expertise, being less concerned about their values alignment. They hired people for their values alignment, being less concerned about their expertise. Going forward, they have decided to hire (at the top of the company) only people who agree with their progressive social values.[5]

▼ The Staples Way.

Staples, the Westboro, Massachusetts–based office supply store chain, has a great way of sustaining a strong customer-service culture using the job-or-no-job philosophy. The company hires new M.B.A.s without having specific jobs for them at the time they are hired. Instead, they hire the person and have him work in different departments until he becomes familiar with and acclimated to the company.

This practice benefits all. First, the company hires a potentially great employee whose values support the company's values. Second, while the M.B.A. holder is working in different departments, the company obtains information about the person's strengths and weaknesses and then uses this to make the best placement decision. Finally, the employee benefits by getting experience in different departments and gaining a better understanding of various parts of the company.

▼ Be Prepared.

Lands' End, the well-known mail-order clothing business in Dodgeville, Wisconsin, offers an unusual benefit to job candidates that clearly demonstrates commitment to the job-or-no-job philosophy. The "job enrollment program" is available to all

Lands' End employees; it allows an employee to train for a job within the company regardless of whether an opening exists for that job. The program is clearly a win-win for all. The employee benefits by learning new skills, and the company benefits by having a workforce that is cross-trained and people who are ready to step into their positions when openings occur.

Staffing Best Practice Six in Action: Multiplicity

Aligned companies involve numerous people in the staffing process and use several methods to screen candidates. This notion of multiplicity represents another way organizations create strong cultural connections and ensure maximum alignment between the company culture and the employee. Here are some examples of how various companies use the best practice of multiplicity in their staffing process.

▼ **Take a Vote.**
Whole Foods Market, located in Austin, Texas, is the largest natural-foods grocer in the United States. It uses decentralized teamwork as a cornerstone of its customer-service culture. To find employees who support that culture, the company links it to hiring practices. Store teams—and only the teams—have the power to approve new hires for full-time jobs. Store leaders screen candidates and recommend them for a job on a specific team. It then takes a two-thirds vote of the team, after what is usually a thirty-day trial period, for the candidate to become a full-time employee.

This hiring approach affects the behavior and attitudes of those involved in the hiring process. Store leaders take great care not to recommend people they do not think the team will approve. Applicants receive a strong message of the importance of teamwork early on in the hiring process. The teams have a voice about their group.

▼ Go Team.

To sustain its innovation-driven culture, 3M has a strong commitment to promoting from within. Most of 3M's staffing practices, therefore, revolve around college recruiting efforts. To most effectively support those efforts, 3M created "focus college relations teams." Again according to Dave Bolles, these teams are currently in place at twenty-eight schools that represent the company's main recruiting sources. The goal of the teams is two-fold: to engage as many people as possible at 3M in recruiting efforts and to better focus the efforts on specific schools.

The teams consist of eight to twelve people representing three functions within the company: engineering, technical, and administrative. Each team organizes all of 3M's recruiting activities at its particular school. The team performs many functions, including:

1. Arranging for professors from the school to work at 3M during the summer in one of their technical areas
2. Coordinating placement of all summer interns
3. Delivering checks for funding a particular project at the school
4. Maintaining consistent and positive relations with the school

These teams develop real pride in representing their university at 3M headquarters. Because they know their school so well, they are able to help the school better understand the benefits of recommending its students to 3M. Because they know 3M so well, they are able to help the company better understand the merits of hiring someone from that particular school.

▼ Play Ball and Rope Cattle.

At spirit-driven Rosenbluth International, niceness counts. The travel company uses several methods to tell who is nice and who is not. One favorite strategy is to ask applicants to play a trial game of softball with the company team. This hiring activity involves employees throughout the organization and gives everyone a good idea of the applicant's overall manner and approach to work.

Another way Rosenbluth incorporates multiplicity into its staffing process is that hiring managers check with all the people a candidate speaks to during a visit, not just the people who interview the candidate. According to the company, one of the best sources of information in this process is the receptionist!

▼ **Informal Innovation.**

W. L. Gore & Associates is in the innovation business. The company develops fluoropolymers for use in filters, dental floss, medical implants, and Gore-Tex fabric. To hire people who support such a culture, a team of interviewers must approve an applicant. The team's questions focus on whether the applicant fits Gore's extremely informal and innovative culture, which lacks organization charts, formal chains of command, titles, and even bosses. Pay increases are based on ratings that employees receive in their biannual peer review. Gore is fanatical about reference checking, calling as many as ten peers, supervisors, and subordinates to evaluate whether a candidate is right for them.

▼ **Share the Wealth.**

Worthington Industries, a steel processor in Columbus, Ohio, shows us how an operationally excellent culture uses the strategy of multiplicity to hire employees who support its culture. All applicants interview with members of a team. If hired, the employee serves a ninety-day probation period and is then voted on by an employee council of ten or so coworkers.

A major reason for the company's heavy emphasis on team potential is that profit sharing accounts for roughly 40 percent of employees' pay at the company. According to Eric Smolenski, a personnel manager at Worthington, "Peers need an opportunity to weigh in on a candidate. They need a chance to ask whether they want to split the pie with a particular individual."[6]

Staffing Best Practice Seven in Action: The Great-Employee Profile

Aligned companies know that they cannot find what they are not looking for. These companies actively and aggressively seek information on their ideal employee. They define the ideal and build their staffing practices to support finding it. Here are some examples of how various companies use the great-employee-profile best practice in their staffing process.

▼ **ESP.**
Several years ago, EMC, a manufacturer of enterprise storage products, realized that it would need to significantly increase staff over the next few years. Top management thought about how the company could add thousands of new people without losing its identity—the cultural attributes that had made it such a success in the first place. A team of senior executives and HR specialists began to ask, What characterizes a great EMC employee? The answer resulted in EMC's "employee success profile." The ESP is a detailed definition of who succeeds at the company. The profile is based on seven critical factors:

1. Technical competence
2. Goal orientation
3. A sense of urgency
4. Accountability
5. External and internal customer responsiveness
6. Cross-functional behavior
7. Integrity

By focusing on these seven attributes, EMC remains much the same company that it was several years ago, even though it has thousands of employees.

▼ A Bunch of Yahoos.

Yahoo, the innovation-driven Internet search company in Santa Clara, California, identified four core attributes of great Yahoo employees:

1. People skills
2. Spheres of influence
3. Zoom in, zoom out
4. Passion for life

People skills, as the name implies, refers to a candidate's interpersonal skills.

Spheres of influence alludes to the candidate's "little black book" of top talent. Because of Yahoo's tremendous growth and because its people know that their current employees are one of their best recruiting tools, they focus not only on the candidate's skills but also on the potential talent that the candidate can bring to the organization.

Yahoo also needs people who can think tactically as well as strategically; they refer to this skill as the ability to "zoom in, zoom out."

Finally, Yahoo wants people who are passionate about their subject area. The company has found that people who are passionate about something specific tend to be passionate about life in general.

▼ Preferred Stock.

Prudential Securities illustrates how a customer-service culture can use the great-employee profile to hire well-suited employees. Prudential examined the kinds of people who are likely to succeed within the company and defined twelve criteria for use in hiring new financial advisers. As part of the hiring process, candidates take a written test for experience, complete a battery of structured interviews, write a financial plan, and visit Prudential offices up to four times. Approximately ten candidates apply for every person hired.

Prudential estimates their investment per hire to be between $60,000 and $100,000. These estimates include costs associated with candidate evaluation, first-year training, and draws against commission. On the other hand, the first round of advisers hired using the twelve criteria exceeded Prudential's expectations by generating an average of $14.5 million of client assets each.

▼ **Reservations, Please.**

Ann Rhoades, executive vice president of human resources at Doubletree Hotels Corporate in Phoenix, worked in conjunction with Development Dimensions International (the human resource consulting firm we met in connection with BMW) to identify the personal attributes of her star performers as well as those employees whose stars were fading—or had already faded. She used this information to create a database of "dimensions for success" so she could search for people who were a good fit.

For example, the success factors identified for reservations agents include practical learning, teamwork, tolerance for stress, sales ability, attention to detail, adaptability/flexibility, and motivation. Doubletree saw these success factors as key in creating superior customer service. Rhoades used the success dimensions to design specific interview questions and exercises to probe for these and other attributes prior to hiring a job candidate.

▼ **The "Skins" Game.**

Walt McGhee of Xerox (introduced earlier under best practice three, "Image Is Everything") built his new channels division by first establishing very specific criteria for his sales recruits. He described his ideal recruits this way: "They had to be solid performers earning between $100,000 and $200,000 a year. They should not be next in line for a promotion at their current company. And they had to have a commitment of 'skin' in the game." In others words, they had to have lots to gain, but something to risk: losing a well-paying job by joining his team.

Although Xerox has not revealed specific figures, it appears McGhee's profile and his recruiting tactics work. Analysts note that the channels division is off to a strong start, and Xerox is expected to introduce some aggressive product lines to show its commitment to the division.

Staffing Best Practice Eight in Action: Beyond Benchmarking

Aligned companies go beyond looking to other companies for the keys to successful staffing. Truly aligned companies know the value of looking inward rather than to their competition for great staffing ideas. By looking inward, they incorporate their knowledge of the culture into staffing practices. Here are some examples of how various companies have gone beyond benchmarking in their staffing process.

▼ **I Dare You.**
The core culture at Cisco Systems is so amazingly innovative that people openly share all their current staffing programs with anyone who asks—including competitors. Why would they be so willing to give away their staffing secrets? They simply follow their employment charter, which reads: "To challenge and outperform all standard and accepted forms of staffing." The consensus within the human resource department is that if the company is turning over its products every six to twelve months, Human Resources should follow this practice as well.

▼ **Creative Abrasion.**
Nissan Design International (NDI), based in LaJolla, Cali-

fornia, creates cars of the future. The auto design studio shows us another great example of how innovation-driven culture uses the beyond-benchmarking strategy to hire people who sustain the company's culture. According to Jerry Hirshberg, NDI's founder and president, "Sometimes the right person for the job is two people." Hirshberg hires people in pairs to create what he calls "creative abrasion." In hiring people to design new cars, creativity is a critical success factor. When it comes to creativity, Hirshberg believes that two people are better than one. Moreover, he's looking for two people who see the world in entirely different ways.

NDI now has more than twenty-five pairs of highly talented, creative, and strong-willed employees. Hiring in divergent pairs has become a defining organizational principle for NDI.

Hirshberg warns other companies considering this hiring approach: "You need to have a pretty strong sense of self when a person working on the same project as you has an entirely different set of priorities. The folks we're hiring share almost nothing—except a deep belief in their own way and their own passion."[7]

▾ **One Question.**

Rather than hiring store managers with previous restaurant experience, the fast-food chain Chick-fil-A, headquartered in Atlanta, focuses its assessment of the candidate on such things as character, drive, and whether or not she has a natural liking for people. Recruiters who hire store managers often ask themselves one key question when evaluating candidates: "Would I like to have my son or daughter working for this person?"

▾ **Live What You Sell.**

Recreational Equipment, Inc. (REI), the nation's largest consumer cooperative of outdoor products, goes far beyond traditional practices associated with hiring employees who can provide good customer service. REI's employees do more than just serve customers by greeting them as they enter the store, answering their questions about various products, and ringing up their purchases. Employees working for any retailer should be able to perform those functions. REI has gone a step beyond by hiring people who live the lifestyle that REI sells. Typical interview questions for hiring store personnel include: "What's your favorite alpine lake? What fishing pole do you carry? What kind of tent do you use?" Hiring people who "live what REI sells" results in a level of customer service unparalleled in most retailers.

▼ **Hey, Pizza Man.**

One more example of how the Cisco Systems culture of innovation permeates potential applicant pools is its well-known pizza campaign. Many great companies give away tons of hats, T-shirts, and logo-laden stuff to potential recruits. Again, Cisco rewrites recruiting by getting inside the heads of students, knowing not only what they need and want but when they need it and want it. Cisco sends pizzas to university residence halls where students are studying for finals, with a note inside the pizza box saying "good luck" and providing a reminder of the Cisco Website (just in case someone wants to apply).

NOTES

1. Kevin Freiberg and Jackie Freiberg, *Nuts: Southwest Airlines' Crazy Recipe for Business and Personal Success* (Austin, Tex.: Bard Press, 1996), pp. 64–73.

2. Tim Ouellette, "Corporate Strategies," www2.computerworld.com/home/print.nsf/All/9803303E56 (March 30, 1998).

3. Julia King, "Corporate Strategies," www2.computerworld.com/home/print9497.nsf/All/SL3bounty (January 20, 1997).

4. Caroline Bollinger, "Building a Sales Force From Scratch," *Sales and Marketing Management*, vol. 15, no. 2 (February 1998), pp. 26–28.

5. Ben Cohen and Jerry Greenfield, *Ben & Jerry's Double-Dip: Lead*

With Your Values and Make Money, Too (New York: Simon & Schuster, 1997), pp. 185–188.

6. Justin Martin, "So, You Want to Work for the Best," *Fortune* (January 12, 1998), pp. 77–78.

7. Katherine Mieszkowski, "Opposites Attract," *Fast Company* (December–January 1998), pp. 42–44.

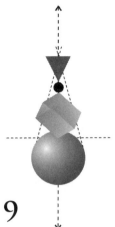

CHAPTER 9

ALIGNING STAFFING TO CORE CULTURE

This chapter provides action ideas to help you begin to align your staffing practices with your core culture. You might want to start by going directly to the section of this chapter that pertains to the core culture of your organization:

- ▼ Customer Service
- ▼ Innovation
- ▼ Operational Excellence
- ▼ Spirit

As you review the action ideas for your culture, consider three questions:

1. How can you implement the action item to improve your ability to find great employees?
2. How does the action item complement existing staffing practices?

3. What additional resources are needed to implement the action idea?

To create additional ideas for aligning your staffing strategies to your core culture, review the action ideas presented for the other cultures. You'll see that many of the same action ideas work for different cultures. The gist of each action is the same across the four categories, but the focus of the particular action differs with the core culture.

CUSTOMER SERVICE CULTURE

The following actions will help you align your staffing practices to your core culture of creating customer solutions.

▼ Rate your staffing process and materials on a scale from 1 to 10 on how well they communicate your customer-service culture connections (reach out and touch, the customer is always the customer, love and marriage, I own the problem, and real-time reactions). Use this information to identify improvement opportunities for your organization's staffing function and materials.

▼ Evaluate your staffing process using the same standards you use to evaluate your external customer-service process (such as positive image, courteousness, responsiveness, response time, quality of interaction, etc.). Determine how well you integrate your customer-service standards into your staffing process.

▼ Examine how well your company responds to all applicants. Ask staffing personnel to each suggest two ways to provide applicants with more immediate, direct, and frequent feedback.

▼ Develop your image of customer service by sponsoring or making presentations at regional and national conferences that focus on customer service.

▼ Profile your superlative customer-service employees in company recruiting materials. Give examples from actual customers about what make these employees great. Include those employees in your staffing process through interviews and other forms of contact with job candidates.

▼ Develop a video or scrapbook that contains employees' descriptions of best, worst, and typical customer-service encounters. Promote real-world presentation of your company by sharing this information with all applicants.

▼ Create a team of marketing, advertising, and human resource representatives to develop staffing materials that reflect a customer-service focus. Treat applicants as customers by including applicants in review and evaluation of these materials.

▼ Develop behaviorally based questions that focus on customer service, and use these questions when interviewing for all positions. Base questions on real-life internal and external customer-service situations.

▼ Identify areas within your organization that need stronger emphasis on customer service. Within the next six months, hire at least one full-time employee in those areas regardless of whether or not you have a specific job opening at the time.

▼ Involve external customers in your staffing process. Ask them to evaluate your staffing materials (classified ads, recruiting brochures, interview questions, etc.) or interview your applicants. For positions that do not directly serve the external customer, have at least one internal customer of that position interview applicants.

▼ Ask applicants what they like best about your company's staffing process and what they would change. To better serve your staffing customers, change your process based on their feedback.

▼ Form multidepartmental recruiting teams to plan, coordinate, and participate in the staffing of a key customer-service position within the company. Involve each team in at least one recruiting event a year.

▼ Interview ten great customer-service employees to uncover what makes it easy to be a top employee, and what makes it difficult. Strengthen and increase those things that make it easy. Remove barriers that keep people from being great customer-service employees.

▼ List three things that your current staffing process does to find employees who connect with your customer-service culture—three things that are not based on actions of your major competitors. Go beyond benchmarking and establish an annual goal to create three to five new staffing processes or sets of materials that help you better identify applicants who connect with your customer-service culture.

▼ Annually survey your employees to obtain ideas on how to improve the company's ability to find employees who connect with your customer-service culture.

INNOVATION CULTURE

The following actions will help you align your staffing practices to your core culture of creating and shaping the future.

▼ Rate your staffing process and materials on a scale from 1 to 10 on how well they communicate your innovation-culture connections (need for speed, cannibalization and creative destruction, freedom to succeed, take it to the limit, have fun and kill the enemy, and the thrill of adventure). Use this information to identify improvement opportunities for your organization's staffing function and materials.

▼ In your staffing materials and process, communicate examples of your organization's hot projects and how they cannibalize, stretch, and create new projects. Describe specific hot projects, and profile employees who played a key role in the innovation required for those projects.

▼ Ask applicants for three ways to radically improve or innovate your staffing process. Incorporate their suggestions and feedback into your staffing activities and materials wherever appropriate.

▼ Assess your organization's "new toys" factor. In your staffing materials and processes, describe the vanguard technology you use to gain a competitive advantage. Profile those of your organization's best toys that are available to employees.

▼ Strengthen your organization's image of innovation by sponsoring or making presentations at regional and national conferences that focus on innovation.

▼ Profile your organization's great innovators in your recruiting materials. Describe specific examples about what makes these employees special. Include your innovators in the staffing process through interviews and other forms of contact with job candidates.

▼ Use e-mail and other innovative communication methods to connect with your applicants. Send a quarterly or biannual communication to applicants, highlighting the company's latest innovations and describing current job opportunities with your company.

▼ Assist elementary and secondary schools in developing your organization's innovators of tomorrow. Sponsor programs and scholarships that support students who have an interest in areas that support your innovation-driven culture.

▼ Identify areas within your organization that need stronger emphasis on innovation. Within the next six months, hire at least one full-time employee in those areas, regardless of whether or not you have a specific job at the time.

▼ Develop behaviorally based questions that focus on innovation, and use these questions when interviewing for all positions. Base questions on real-life innovation situations at your company.

▼ Use at least two methods (application, interview, test, etc.) to assess applicants' ability to connect with your innovation culture. Make sure that each method assesses at least three of the six cultural connections (need for speed, cannibalization and creative destruction, freedom to succeed, take it to the limit, have fun and kill the enemy, thrill of adventure).

▼ Designate a representative from the company to be a liaison to contacts at local businesses that support innovation (inventor associations, patent lawyers, etc.). Provide these groups with company information for them to distribute to their members or clients. Sponsor at least one of their meetings every year.

▼ Interview ten great innovative employees to uncover what makes it easy to be a top employee, and what makes it difficult. Strengthen and increase those things that make it easy. Remove barriers that keep people from being highly innovative employees.

▼ List three things that your current staffing process does to find employees who connect with your innovation culture—three things that are not based on actions of your major competitors. Go beyond benchmarking by establishing an annual goal to create three to five new staffing processes or sets of materials that help you better identify applicants who connect with your innovation-driven culture.

▼ Annually survey your employees on how to improve the company's ability to find employees who connect with your innovation-driven culture.

OPERATIONAL EXCELLENCE CULTURE

The following actions will help you align your staffing practices to your core culture of creating processes that minimize costs and maximize productivity.

▼ Rate your staffing process and materials on a scale from 1 to 10 on how well they communicate your operational-excellence culture connections (standardize; get it right; measure twice, cut once; stay within the lines that are our friends; and waste not, want not). Use this information to identify improvement opportunities for your organization's staffing function and materials.

▼ Evaluate your staffing process using the same quality standards and metrics (such as reject rates, number of errors, production rates, etc.) that you use to evaluate other functions within the company. Make sure processes are consistent across locations, and eliminate any waste in staffing process in terms of time or money.

▼ Develop your image of operational excellence by publishing (in national business and trade publications) stories on your latest advances in this area of work and the employees involved.

▼ Profile your operationally excellent employees in company recruiting materials. Describe specific examples of what makes these employees great. Include them in your staffing process through interviews and other forms of contact with job candidates.

▼ When establishing annual staffing goals, strive to improve the consistency and efficiency of your process. Treat applicants as customers by asking them to identify parts of the process that are redundant or overly time consuming.

▼ Get real with applicants by giving them a tour of the facility or area where they will work. Use this time to discuss the operationally excellent culture connections (standardize; get it right; measure twice, cut once; stay within the lines; waste not, want not).

▼ Identify areas within your organization that need stronger emphasis on operational excellence. Within the next six months, hire at least one full-time employee in those areas regardless of whether or not you have a specific job at that time.

▼ Develop behaviorally based questions that focus on operational excellence, and use these questions when interviewing for all positions. Base questions on real-life situations involving operational excellence that have occurred in your company.

▼ Create a team of your exceptional employees (from the point of view of operational excellence). Involve various members of the team in job fairs, interviewing, and other staffing activities.

▼ In recruiting materials and interviews with all applicants, highlight the significant "Herbies" that your organization has recently overcome. Ask employees who were involved in those efforts to briefly speak with or interview all applicants.

▼ Form multidepartmental recruiting teams to plan, coordinate, and participate in staffing a key operational-excellence position within the company. Involve each team in at least one recruiting event a year.

▼ Profile ten great employees (in terms of operational excellence) to uncover what makes it easy to be a top employee, and what makes it difficult. Strengthen or increase those things that make it easy. Remove barriers that keep people from being great.

▼ Ask long-term, high-performing employees about what they feel are the strongest operational-excellence culture connections to the company and to their jobs. Profile employees' comments in your recruiting materials and during the interview process.

▼ Ask applicants to attend company events where employees are recognized for their contributions to operational excellence. Ask those employees being recognized to speak with and spend time with applicants.

▼ Evaluate your selection process to determine the multiple methods you use to identify applicants' ability to connect with your operationally excellent culture. Make sure you assess applicants based on the five cultural connections (standardize; get it right; measure twice, cut once; stay within the lines; waste not, want not).

SPIRIT CULTURE

The following actions will help you align your staffing practices to your core culture of creating an environment that supports employees.

▼ Rate your staffing process and materials on a scale from 1 to 10 on how well they communicate your innovation-culture connections (servant leadership; work for a greater good; build people first; faith, hope, and charity; beyond the bottom line; and competitive yet humane). Use this information to identify improvement opportunities for your organization's staffing function and materials.

▼ Develop your image of spirit by sponsoring at least one local or regional event that reflects your company's religious-based, socially based, or employee-based spirit.

▼ Invite applicants to attend one of your company's spirit-related activities (such as celebration of a company milestone, a company-sponsored volunteer day, etc.).

▼ Develop a "friends and family" employee referral program, encouraging employees to refer friends and family members for various job openings.

▼ Create a video or book describing your company's "history of spirit." Describe past efforts related to sustaining your culture of spirit. Share this information with all applicants.

▼ Identify areas within your organization that need stronger emphasis on spirit. Within the next six months, hire at least one full-time employee in those areas regardless of whether or not you have a specific job at the time.

▼ Develop behaviorally based questions that focus on your organization's spirit, and use these questions when interviewing for all positions. Base questions on real-life situations involving company spirit.

▼ Profile company events in recruiting materials and interviews that best exemplify your organization's spirit.

▼ Partner with organizations (religious-based or socially based) that complement your company's culture of spirit. Provide the organization with information about the company to share with its volunteers. Obtain information about the organization so as to encourage all applicants to volunteer or support them.

▼ Form multidepartmental recruiting teams to plan, coordinate, and participate in staffing a key spirit position within the company. Involve each team in at least one recruiting event a year.

▼ Designate a spirit leader, preferably a long-term, high-performing employee who embodies your organization's spirit. Ask him to speak with or interview all applicants focusing on your company's culture of spirit.

▼ Profile ten great employees of spirit to uncover what makes it easy to be a top employee, and what makes it difficult. Strengthen or increase those things that make it easy. Remove barriers that keep people from being exceptional employees of spirit.

▼ To send a message regarding your company's commitment to servant leadership, require employees involved in the staffing process to serve the applicant in at least one way during the process. The employee can offer applicants coffee or soda, provide them with a coupon for a free lunch in the company cafeteria, validate their parking permit, and so on.

▼ In your staffing materials and interviews, describe your company's efforts to build people first. Focus on the company's efforts to train, support, and nurture all employees.

▼ Survey your employees annually on how to improve the company's ability to find people who connect with your spirit-driven culture.

▼ ▼ ▼

The action ideas in this chapter are general and are meant to provide only a starting point for your own efforts at alignment. Because you have a lot more information about your company and its culture, we strongly encourage you to create unique action ideas to best align your staffing materials and processes to your company's core culture.

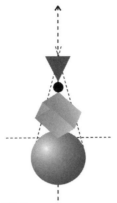

PART FOUR

KEEPING GREAT EMPLOYEES

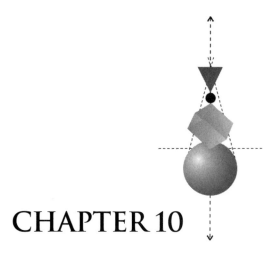

CHAPTER 10

RETENTION BEST PRACTICES

Here's a little secret. Your best staffing plan is to create a great retention plan! Today's "best" companies understand that the real key to maintaining a world-class workforce is not to just hire the best, but to keep them once they are hired. They focus the same effort on keeping great employees as they do on finding great employees. With the same tenacity, attention to detail, and "salesmanship" they use to attract great employees, these companies consistently retain far greater numbers of key employees than their competitors do.

EIGHT BEST PRACTICES IN RETENTION

Regardless of the core culture, be it customer service, innovation, operational excellence, or spirit, world-class organizations integrate eight best-practice strategies into the fabric of the company.

Retention Best Practice One: Engage the Soul

As you walk into most organizations today, you sense an over-powering absence of something. Although sometimes hard to describe, the missing thing is nevertheless so palpable that internal employees have become hardened to it. Gleaned from the lifeless eyes of employees, or the pin-dropping quietness in the hallways, you have entered yet another organization that has lost its heart, its life, its soul. Though the employees don't sense it, outside guests invariably respond—sadly—to the realization.

Soulless bureaucracies dominate the workplace. They come in every size and shape imaginable, from small family-owned businesses to multinational global enterprises. They are just as common in the public sector as in the private sector, and they do not discriminate by industry, geography, or service. Sadly yet predictably, they are fertile breeding grounds for massive disconnection.

Disconnections abound within soulless bureaucracies. Management in the wasteland fervently clings to the hopelessly outdated belief that business is no place for humanness, that buying a person's hands and head is more important than engaging a person's heart and soul. Employees trapped within such systems perform to the bare minimum standards, rising only to the level of management's forced compliance. Such workplaces deaden the spirits of workers everywhere. But they also offer progressive, aligned companies a magnificent competitive opportunity!

Aligned companies enthusiastically find ways to engage the very hearts and souls of their employees. They embrace the wisdom of the great prophet who said, "For what will a man profit if he gains the whole world but loses his soul?" Great employees naturally search out, join, and stay with organizations that give them compelling reasons to commit their hearts and souls to something beyond quarterly stock reports or annual plans.

Powerful connections abound within organizations that engage the souls of their workers. Such aligned companies clearly understand that imagination, creativity, and a passion for excellence all reside not in the mind but in the soul. They also realize that to engage the souls of workers is not an esoteric experiment or an attempt at crystal-ball futurism. Rather, it is a direct, creative, and results-based strategy that unleashes a powerful and deep connection between the employee and the employer, a connection that creates high retention rates among great employees. These connections leapfrog many traditional, skin-deep attempts to motivate workers through slogans and banners, instead developing strategic actions that inspire long-term employee excellence. In creative, interesting, and exciting ways, aligned companies forge connections with employees that touch their hearts and engage their souls.

Retention Best Practice Two: What Gets Rewarded Gets Done

This ever-so-basic management principle easily gets lost within our complicated, fast-paced business world. Many fine companies lose sight of the basic tenet that whatever they reward becomes the focal point for most employee behavior. Employees quickly learn what is and is not important to the company by how they are recognized and rewarded—and reprimanded. Praise and congratulations for a certain behavior encourages that behavior. Reprimands and punishment for other behaviors quickly extinguish.

Top-performing companies align their rewards to the core culture. They realize that the stronger the connection between reward systems and core culture, the greater the productivity of employees. Whether having at their core customer service, innovation, operational excellence, or spirit, aligned companies most often reward what is most important to the culture.

When rewards and culture do not align, employee disconnections result. A company that claims to be innovation-driven but primarily rewards operational excellence sends mixed messages. Should employees focus on creating the future, or on staying within the lines? Should employees spend more time and energy on elevating the core culture of innovation to a new level, or on dealing with process control issues?

Aligned companies concentrate on how and what reward systems best drive their culture to new levels and then weave these reward systems into the very fabric of the culture. The sometimes obvious (awards, bonuses, incentives) and sometimes subtle (a thank-you from the boss) reward systems build strong company-to-employee connections. They also build strong employee-to-company connections through allowing employees to be recognized for helping sustain a robust corporate culture.

Retention Best Practice Three: More Than Money

Is money important to us? Of course, because without it, none of us could survive. But is money the most important motivator for doing what we do?

In our experience, for the vast majority of employees money is not the primary motivator. Something deeper inspires employee excellence, something that connects to the employee in a personal way. Endless surveys conclude that money is seldom ranked as the main reason for joining, leaving, or contributing one's best to a company. Yet as soon as most nonaligned companies realize a great employee is about to leave, their automatic reflex is to throw dough at him in the hope that he will stick around.

Nonaligned organizations with no retention strategy tied to core culture disproportionately rely upon money and monetary incentives in their attempts to retain top employees. These reactive efforts to blackmail great employees into staying with the company often backfire, resulting in demoralized and disconnected staff. Nonaligned companies fail to realize that by the time a great employee decides to leave, she is already so disconnected that most attempts to bribe her to stay will fail. Even if the bribe works and the employee stays, the company now has a highly paid but disconnected employee who has the opportunity to further disconnect other great employees from the core culture.

Aligned companies embrace what Bill Silberman, a seasoned compensation and benefits executive and currently president of Green Tree Consulting in Seminole, Florida, calls the "intangible benefits of membership." According to Silberman, in building world-class retention strategies it is far more important today to focus on the intangible benefits of company membership (pride in organizational brand, pride in being part of something important, career development, team spirit) than on the tangible benefits (traditional pay and benefit plans). Further, he says that a well-crafted strategy of intangible benefits "demonstrates that the organization values the employee's professional, physical, mental, and spiritual well-being," which is a powerful and effective retention technique for great employees.

Aligned organizations recognize that great employees sustain world-class performance more from their passionate connection to the core culture than from a passionate need for money. Their use of monetary incentives is part (though a relatively small one) of their total retention equation. A primary focus is to build an overall retention strategy that deeply connects to something more than an employee's bank account. Creative programs are developed to retain superior employees through meaningful connections to core culture and purpose.

Retention Best Practice Four: Learning Drives Earning

Hanging over the entrance to the Du Pont Center for Human Development in Wilmington, Delaware, is a plaque that reads, "The competitive advantage belongs to the organization that can decrease the cycle time of learning and apply learning to work." In today's economy, everyone is a knowledge worker. Brainpower has replaced brute power as the primary means of productivity. Intellectual capital has replaced financial capital as the key to competitive advantage. The learning organization has replaced reengineering as a key strategic initiative.

Employees understand all too well that their very livelihood depends upon the ability to learn. They recognize that they must exponentially grow their own intellectual capital to survive. Within a world of massive change and lightning-fast technological advances, employees embrace opportunities to aggressively flex and develop their skills. Yet there are two significant roadblocks facing most employees, over which they have little control.

The first roadblock faced by employees who desire to grow their learning takes the form of an organization that refuses to invest significant dollars in training. It pays lip service to employee training but claims that "training is too expensive," "it's not in the budget," "there's no time," or "if we train them, they'll just leave." We suggest that if you *don't* train them, the best *do* leave, and in turn only mediocre talent remains. Such organizations die a quick death in our knowledge-based global economy.

The second obstacle faced by employees desiring to grow their learning is the organization that does not align the learning to core culture. Training and development programs are often delivered with no relationship to the core culture, no direct tie to the core reason for corporate existence. Programs and seminars are thrown at employees—sometimes improving skills and knowledge, but having little impact on operational performance. Why? Training has no clear, concrete connection to the core culture.

Aligned companies reap the benefits of a knowledge-rich workforce. Companies filled with knowledge-rich employees who clearly understand how and why their knowledge ties into core culture always outperform nonaligned companies. Employees within aligned companies understand that culture-based learning improves company performance, which in turn improves chances for personal earning. Therefore, the greater the employee's potential earning capacity, the greater the retention.

Retention Best Practice Five: Get a Life

Not too many years ago, the good life was perceived as getting on the fast track of business: Work hard, strike the deal, hit the road, make the bonus, impress the boss, move up the ladder. There was little time for anything beyond closing the big deal or finishing the big project. Even though we were pushed to the edge, we were told by friends (and the message was reinforced through countless media advertisements) that yes, we could have it all. But somewhere along the way, the fast track lost its gleam. Its promises of fame, fortune, and happiness were replaced with the startling realities of massive stress, relationship upheavals, and career burnout.

The fast track has lost much of its luster in recent years. Those who jumped on the bandwagon, as well as those who merely stood by and observed, now realize that the fast track is not the right track for everyone. In fact, for many great employees, the drive to get on the fast track has been replaced with a drive to get on with a life, one that focuses just as much (and maybe more) on what happens outside of work than on what happens at work.

Balancing work and personal life is and will continue to be a tremendous challenge for all employers. With the competitive pressure to produce higher qualities and quantities of work every day, with fewer and fewer workers, organizations walk a tough path. On the one hand, they must demand an ever-increasing amount of time, commitment, and energy from their employees to remain competitive. On the other hand, they must somehow balance their business needs with their employees' yearning for better overall quality of life. Push too hard, and the organization may win, but the employee may lose. Fail to push hard enough, and the employee may win, but the organization may lose.

Work-life integration remains a critically important element of strategic retention. Progressive, aligned companies such as Xerox, the SAS Institute, and Fel-Pro understand that retention of great employees significantly hinges upon their ability to allow employees to regain a sense of control over both their work and personal lives.

Aligned companies help integrate the outside personal life of the worker with his or her inside organizational life. They see strategic retention as more than just making an employee's worklife more bearable, and more than just streamlining an employee's work schedule. Through blending employees' personal lives into the very fabric of the culture, aligned organizations further loyalty and retention of great employees. It is their burning desire that every employee, from the CEO to the frontline clerk, get a life!

Retention Best Practice Six: In the Loop

Remember the last time you sensed you were out of the corporate loop? Remember how you felt uninformed, and unimportant? At one time or another, we have all believed we were disconnected from our company. This disconnection tears at the very heart of our allegiance to our colleagues, our department, and the company at large. Disconnected employees feel out of the loop of vital internal information flow so necessary for contributing to world-class performance.

The fastest way to transform a top-performing staff into a group of disgruntled, discouraged, job-seeking workers is to shut them out of the loop of corporate information. Struggling companies often learn this painful lesson too late. They fail to understand that if information is power, then they must share it at all organizational levels. Attempting to hoard information is a losing proposition within our knowledge-rich world.

Aligned companies understand that in-the-loop employees feel strong connections to the company. Connected employees jump into major projects, freely contribute their ideas and energy, and recommit themselves to the company goals. They are more willing to take on additional work and go the extra mile for the company. In each case, a stronger connection to the company is made through feeling that one is in the loop.

A critical key to successful retention is to tie communication to the core culture. Company communications—whether on financial performance, competitor analysis, internal announcements, or just general information—must reinforce the core corporate culture to employees. Wonderful opportunities exist to reinforce and drive the culture by way of internal communications that in turn yield higher retention.

Retention Best Practice Seven: Lighten Up

Without question, one of the most disheartening aspects of business today is that so many organizations continue to take themselves far too seriously. Their cold, stoic, and impersonal style—"the serious business of business is serious business"—forces employees to check their hearts and their laughter at the door. Such organizations squelch any attempts by employees to bring their naturally fun-loving, upbeat personalities into the workplace. It's as if a huge banner containing a slight revision to

Dante's memorable proclamation hangs over the entrance to the Inferno, reading: "Abandon all humor, ye who enter here."

One clear distinction generally exists between aligned and nonaligned organizations. Aligned organizations take their work—but not themselves—very seriously. This subtle distinction often separates the great organizations from the mediocre. Make a short list of the companies that immediately come to mind that are unafraid, even proud, to allow people to lighten up. It is likely to include such powerhouses as Southwest Airlines, Ben & Jerry's, Disney, and Sun Microsystems. Not surprisingly, this list also represents companies with high retention rates within their respective industries.

Aligned organizations understand that great employees are sure to remain with a company that is not afraid to lighten up. They passionately pursue creating an environment that reinforces to employees that it's OK to be yourself, to share the humor of your daily struggles, to be a little silly, to find the lighter side of business, and to share your heart! Great employees are magnetically connected to organizations that lighten up and have a little fun.

Retention Best Practice Eight: Free at Last

"Free-agent nation" is what *Fast Company* magazine recently heralded on its cover as the reality of corporate America. Their claim: that every employee is a free agent and should approach his or her career as an independent, solo artisan. If this is true (and even if it is not), how can corporations build long-term employee retention into their everyday operations?

Perhaps the greatest irony in world-class retention practices is that the greater the employee freedom, the greater the retention. Traditional management thinking abhors the idea of allowing employees freedom to control their work. Yet in today's market, anything less than allowing employees a wide range of operational latitude significantly diminishes an organization's ability to be fast, flexible, and responsive where it really counts: on the front line.

In far too many organizations, bureaucracy smothers common sense. Well-meaning rules and regulations often demotivate rather than inspire employees. Further, seldom do such rules tie into and promote the core culture. Rather, they impede and slow down progress, and generally lead to stagnation.

Powerful connections occur when companies give employees the protection they need to excel—the power to control their own destinies—and then get out of their way. Top employees thrive within environments that allow maximum operational freedom. Even within quality or operational-excellence cultures, where regulations and process are king, world-class companies allow employees great leeway in solving problems on the front line without "kicking it upstairs."

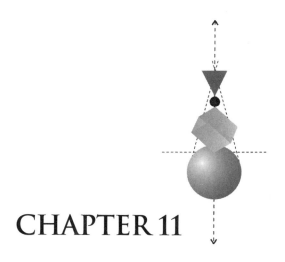

CHAPTER 11

RETENTION BEST PRACTICES IN ACTION

There are no secrets to retaining great employees, except that it is hard, focused work. Aligned companies willingly expend the energy and commitment necessary to retain top employees because they realize that the best labor pool is often the one they have already developed. Rather than going along with non-aligned companies that generally look outside the organization to locate top talent, aligned organizations look internally to retain employees who are already performing at superior levels. Aligned organizations therefore have a twofold competitive advantage: They find great employees when they need them and they keep the ones they have.

PUTTING WHAT'S BEST INTO ACTION

Regardless of their core culture, aligned companies integrate each of the eight best practices into their retention strategies.

Since one of the goals of this book is to help you create an action plan to better align your retention strategies to core culture, please heed the following advice. As you read the many examples within each best-practice category, ask yourself three questions:

1. How do you currently integrate the eight best practices into your retention strategies?
2. How might the essence of each example be integrated into your current retention plan?
3. What would you have to modify, expand, eliminate, or create to integrate these examples into your existing programs?

Through answering these questions, you jump-start your action plan preparation and are that much closer to aligning your retention strategies to core culture.

Best Practice One in Action: Engage the Soul

Aligned organizations actively engage the hearts and souls of the best employees. Through integrating specific soul-engaging action ideas into the very fabric of their culture, aligned organizations unleash the energy, enthusiasm, and creativity of great employees. Here are some examples of how aligned companies engage the soul of employees.

▼ Just Imagine Drive.

Even as you approach the specialty building materials maker in Westlake, Ohio, the intent to engage the soul is evident—to enter Manco's facilities, you must drive your car down Just Imagine Drive! CEO Jack Kahl understands that only through a fully engaged workforce can Manco fulfill its compelling mission to "compete against the giants." And who might the giants be? None other than the likes of Minnesota Mining and Manufacturing, better known as 3M. Think of the effect of driving each day into and out of a worksite that reminds you to "just imagine." Through appealing to the very souls of his employees, Kahl reminds his midsize company to just imagine beating 3M.

▼ **Not Your Charlie Chaplin.**

A movement is sweeping through the spirit-driven cultures in American business, not of engaging the souls of employees by showing them Charlie Chaplin movies, but through comforting their souls with the influence of "workplace chaplains." Hundreds of fine organizations (whether embracing a spirit-driven culture or not) are contracting with independent workplace chaplain consulting services. Generally rolled into their normal employee assistance programs, progressive organizations offer a broad range of religious counselors, including priests, rabbis, ministers, and monks. Such broad-based use of workplace chaplains allows these organizations to meet the growing spiritual needs of their increasingly diverse workforce.

▼ **Forty Hours a Year.**

Timberland, the successful New Hampshire footwear manufacturer, is a fine example of how a culture of operational excellence engages the souls of workers with activities outside of work itself. Timberland allows every employee to donate up to forty hours a year to outside corporate or individual projects. Deep connections to Timberland result through its willingness to allow employees an opportunity to share their skills, knowledge, and passion with groups that touch their souls. Many employees join in corporate-sponsored trips to Puerto Rico, for example, to participate in various habitat and human service projects throughout the island.

▼ **Keys to the Soul.**

Engaging the soul need not focus on saving the world—or even saving a soul. Innovation-driven SAS, a computer software company in Carey, North Carolina, engages a pianist to play during lunch hours. By allowing the musician to softly stroke the keys, SAS softly strokes the souls of its employees, building a subtle yet soothing employee connection.

▼ **No Hidden Agendas.**

When it comes to hidden agendas, spirit-driven Advanced Technology Consultants does not believe in them. The Atlanta provider of communications software proudly shares with applicants and employees that their mission is "serving God while bringing people and technology together." With such a refreshingly candid and honest approach, Advanced Technology Consultants both attracts and retains employees who believe in and share a similar personal mission.

▼ **Passion Plaque.**

Kingston Computers, a Fountain Valley, California, high-tech manufacturer, ignites a passionate connection to employees' souls via its "passion plaque." Displayed in the lobby, the magnificent plaque lists the four core goals to which all employees must aspire and are held accountable at Kingston: "courtesy, compassion, modesty, and honesty." Thus Kingston engages the souls of employees through a constant reminder of what is most important to its success—and what connects so deeply to the soul for them.

Best Practice Two in Action: What Gets Rewarded Gets Done

Aligned organizations know that what gets rewarded gets done. They create innovative ways to retain top-flight employees through connecting rewards to the core culture. Here are several progressive organizations that further retention through culturally aligned reward systems.

▼ **Equal Weighting.**

Rick Valines, the vice president of human resources at Griffen Industries of Cold Springs, Kentucky, recognized that turnover was far too high notwithstanding the company's culture of operational excellence in manufacturing. So Valines redesigned the performance review process that determines managers' raises and bonuses. The new review elevated the importance of turnover, giving it equal weight with such other areas as quality and safety. Not surprisingly, turnover quickly went down. Managers are now concentrating on making long-term connections with the best employees—and all it took at Griffen was equal weighting.

▼ **Ten Percent and 40 Percent.**

Customer service and customer solutions are a significant part of Metamor Technologies' quarterly bonus system. Four times a year within this Chicago-based customer-service consulting company, supervisors call all forty clients and ask if they are satisfied with Metamor's communication, ability to solve problems, and responsiveness to needs; they also ask about the customer's willingness to give a reference. With up to 10 percent of salary and 40 percent of bonuses resting on the answers, Metamor extends its service philosophy into how employees get rewarded. At last count, the average contract has increased tenfold within the last five years, and 75 percent of current clients give their friends unsolicited testimonials on the high level of Metamor's services.

▼ **Customer Goals.**

Great customer-service companies base their rewards on more than just service. GSD&M, an advertising agency in Austin, Texas, boasts a 90 percent client retention rate within an industry known for fast and frequent client turnover. With such large and demanding clients as Wal-Mart and Southwest Airlines, GSD&M connects employees' desire to offer customer solutions with its cutting-edge bonus structure. Rather than set bonuses according to employees' meeting internally driven company goals, GSD&M bases bonuses on how well they help client companies meet their goals.

▼ "I'm Satisfied!"

Even Hallmark Cards of Kansas City implements incentive pay plans based on customer satisfaction. The innovation-driven company's cross-functional, team-based plan is based on customer satisfaction, profitability as measured against budgeted goals, and sales at the retail level—not sales to the retailer. Managers and exempt employees put 10 percent of their pay at risk; all others do so with 5 percent of their pay. The upside is the chance to earn between 12.5 percent and 25 percent more than under previous reward systems. The new system is based primarily upon satisfying the customers and helping them meet their goals.

▼ Get on the Train.

Omron Electronics of Chicago takes a simple, direct, and high-impact approach to ensuring that all managers focus on individual and team training. Sales managers know that 10 percent of pay is tied to meeting ongoing training goals. It is pretty straightforward: If you want to get people on the training train, reward the activity.

Best Practice Three in Action: More Than Money

Aligned organizations recognize that long-term employee retention is built upon more than money. Through a concerted focus beyond short-term monetary gain, aligned organizations engender strong employee connection based upon creative ties to the core culture. Here are some examples of how progressive organizations foster retention through culturally aligned systems that focus on more than money.

▼ Employee Exchange Program.

The spirit-driven management at Rhino Foods of Burlington, Vermont, builds high retention through its employee exchange program. During slow times of the year, Rhino's employees (recognized by the community as some of the best in their area) are "loaned" to other local companies for a maximum of six weeks. This enables Rhino employees to continue earning income during routinely off-peak business times. The power of this example extends well beyond the money each employee earns during the employee exchange program. It is a prime reason for the track record of tremendous loyalty and retention at Rhino Foods.

▼ Horsing Around.

Recognizing that great employees are motivated by more than money, service-driven Computer System Development, a consulting company in Albuquerque, offers unusual incentives for employee success. Based upon what they call "challenge sheets," employees design annual personal and professional goals. In keeping with their western heritage, founder Frank Bohac's employees are often awarded vacations, computers—and even horses.

▼ The Ring's the Thing.

Once a year, the top innovators at 3M are inducted into its Circle of Technical Excellence. Without question, this is the most prestigious honor bestowed upon 3M's top performers. To make the honor quite visible, each recipient is given a Super Bowl–type ring large enough that others cannot help but notice.

Go ahead, try and convince the winners at 3M that the ring is not the thing!

▼ **Everybody Wins.**

At NetManage, a Cupertino, California, software manufacturer, when sales goals are reached everyone in the office wins. Virtually all staff are invited to go on vacation trips to resorts. Within such a spirit-driven culture, great company sales are considered an effort for the entire workforce team. Therefore, the whole team is rewarded. More than 750 employees and guest were included in the last trip.

▼ **Bean Stock.**

Starbucks is as well known for its wonderful benefits packages (for a largely part-time workforce) as for the spirit-driven culture. The employee stock option plan is internally known as their "bean stock" program, where a part-time partner earning six or seven dollars an hour can—in as little as five years—earn enough for a down payment on a house. Stock options and health insurance including dental benefits are offered to all employees.

▼ **Personal Time Donation.**

Cray Research of Eagan, Minnesota, created a powerful program that strengthened the sense of connection among employees. Called the emergency personal-time donation program, it allows any regular full-time or part-time employee to donate between eight and forty hours of accumulated personal time to workers who have less than forty hours of personal time off remaining. An employee-generated idea, it has resulted in donation so far of more than 1,000 hours. All donations of time remain anonymous.

Best Practice Four in Action: Learning Drives Earning

Aligned organizations know that employee learning leads to long-term employee earning. They find progressive ways to retain great employees through connecting employees' lifelong learning to the core culture. Here are several ways aligned organizations promote retention through culturally aligned learning.

▼ **$400 a Year.**

Applewood Plumbing, the progressive service-driven plumbing, heating, and air conditioning services company in Denver that we discussed in Chapter 8, takes an interesting approach to encouraging learning. Founder John Ward pays his technicians up to $400 a year to having plumbing, heating, and cooling repairs made to their own homes—by direct competitors. Their $400 a year allowance gives Applewood's technicians a distinct competitive advantage, learning firsthand the techniques of competitors—from telephone communication style to dispute resolution—and more important, they uncover opportunities to serve their customers even better.

▼ **Get Out of Here.**

Many exemplary companies with service-driven cultures understand that the best way (indeed, the only way) to learn what customers experience in using their products or services is to get out and use them. L. L. Bean pays its employees for outdoor wilderness days spent skiing, hiking, boating, or fishing. The learning derived from seeing, feeling, and living how the customer uses and abuses its products drives the earning potential of great employees. Transferring such hands-on knowledge into their work, employees are far better equipped to offer well-founded, reliable customer advice, which boosts customer loyalty and in turn improves employee earning potential.

▼ **Blue Ribbon Tours.**

In the majority of operational-excellence cultures, the two most frightening words imaginable are "corporate audit." At PSS/World Medical, employees cheer, whoop, and holler whenever their branch is picked for the annual audit. Called the "blue ribbon tours," the audit finds CEO Pat Kelly and other senior staff visiting each branch location and grading it on an extensive yes-no checklist. It includes the top 100 things every branch must do to be successful. The payoff for a high-scoring visit can be considerable. Every employee at the top-scoring branch for the year receives $3,000; employees at the second-highest–scoring branch receive $2,000 each, and so forth, down as far as the number-ten branch, where each employee receives $500.

What generates real learning is that all the nonwinning branches must pay for the top ten branch winnings. This averages about $3,000 taken from the bottom line of every nonwinning branch. Although not a significant amount, it's enough for every branch manager to notice and want to work hard so that it won't happen again next year. Learning how to effectively implement all 100 items thus has an impact on the earning of literally every employee at the Jacksonville, Florida–based PSS/World Medical.

▼ **Two-Minute Warnings.**

At the Phelps Group, a Santa Monica, California, marketing agency, employees are given a two-minute warning at exactly 9:28 A.M. every Monday. They have just enough time to make the weekly staff meeting. Held in an open area, the first order of business is to give away $100 to an employee (picked at random) who can answer a question from the employee handbook. This quick, easy, and fun example boosts earning for all those who learn the employee handbook and motivates learning to the entire Phelps team on critical issues.

▼ **Impact Vote.**

During her staff meetings, Susan Groenwald, president of Barter Corporation in Oakbrook Terrace, Illinois, asks employees to share tales of exemplary customer-service acts performed by other employees. After hearing and learning of the many great service actions taken by colleagues, the fifty-some employees vote on the one customer service act having the greatest impact on the company. The winner receives a cash reward. One of the real payoffs is the enthusiastic connections made between employees and the company; but perhaps the biggest payoff is the many wonderful customer-service anecdotes her sales staff can then share in wooing potential clients—a huge earnings opportunity for the entire staff.

▼ **Twenty-Two Courses.**

At Chaparral Steel, an internationally known specialty steel manufacturer based in Midlothian, Texas, twenty-two classes are offered and open to every employee. Employees within this operational excellence culture are encouraged to learn all the other jobs in their department and are given twenty dollars for each four-hour training course they take on their own time. Employee pay increases as they complete more classes. By supporting employees' long-term learning through both encouragement and incentives, Chaparral has increased work coverage thanks to extensive cross-training and has built a strong retention connection with all levels of staff.

▼ **The Leesburg Experience.**

New hires at Xerox Business Services (XBS, winner of the Malcolm Baldrige award) quickly learn the importance the company places on quality and operational excellence. New account associates, the men and women in charge of onsite customer service, are flown to XBS's international document university in Leesburg, Virginia, for a four-day program on quality. These seven-dollar-an-hour new hires are amazed that XBS cares enough about them and their careers to send them to such a weeklong session on a beautiful campus so soon after joining. By sharing what insiders call "the Leesburg experience," XBS begins to build a long-term relationship with new employees that is built upon a connection to operational excellence.

Best Practice Five in Action: Get a Life

Aligned companies understand that to retain great employees they must focus on finding ways to integrate the demands of work and life. Here are some innovative ways that aligned companies encourage employee retention through helping employees get a life.

▼ **Please Go Away.**
Outstanding performers at investment banker Shulman Associates of Boca Raton, Florida, are given an envelope marked "Please go away." Enclosed in the envelope are airline tickets for spending Christmas in the Bahamas. Shulman reinforces the need for its employees to get a life through this fun and interesting technique that any culture can successfully adopt.

▼ **Take a Hike.**
If you work for Hewlett-Packard (innovation-driven), or Pacific Gas and Electric (customer-driven), you are apt to hear someone tell you to take a hike. That is, take a hike at HP's free cabins or at one of PG&E's seven camping sites. Regardless of core culture type, it is important to occasionally suggest that employees take a hike!

▼ **"Cognoid" Perseverance.**
Any "Cognoid"—the affectionate term used to describe employees at wildly successful, wildly fun Cognex (a Natick, Massachusetts, manufacturer of machine vision systems)—is eligible for a slew of magnificent get-aways if he's the persevering type. For five years of employment, Cognoids are rewarded with a fully paid, three-day getaway to entertainment centers such as Nashville, Orlando, or New Orleans. After ten years of perseverance, Cognoids receive an all-expenses paid vacation to places on the order of London and Paris. After fifteen years, Cognoids

can choose a trip to a designated "wonder of the world," including the Pyramids or the Grand Canyon. Warning: Only those who have a passion for fun will persevere (survive) within this innovation-driven culture.

▼ It's Your Schedule.

Recently at the Xerox customer service center in Dallas, managers took what appeared to be a drastic gamble. They allowed employees to arrange their work schedules almost entirely according to their personal life schedules. The results were just as dramatic as the risk. Absenteeism dropped 30 percent and productivity increased.

▼ High Chairs.

Parents working at the Freddie Mac (FNMA) mortgage offices in McLean, Virginia, can bring their children into the cafeteria at lunchtime. High chairs and booster seats are available.

▼ A Complex Arrangement.

Quad/Graphics, the operationally excellent Wisconsin magazine publisher, recently built a $5 million apartment complex outside its plant in Lomira. Initially designed as a recruitment device—a way to provide affordable housing to younger workers—it can also be considered a great retention device for older Quad/Graphics workers. Here's why: Many of the units are held to provide housing for young employees whose parents also work at Quad/Graphics! Imagine the connection to Quad/Graphics among parents who have helped move their kids into a job and an apartment. Such a complex arrangement continues to generate high employee retention at this perennially well-performing company.

▼ Picture This.

At Kendle, a Cincinnati-based clinical test designer, all 280-some employees were photographed with symbols of their favorite outside-of-work activity. The photographs were then posted all over offices. Kendle found that this was a great way to remind current employees to get a life outside of work. But they discovered an unexpected surprise from posting these photographs: It was also a great recruiting tool for prospective employees. The photographs demonstrate that there is and should be life outside of work, and they allow prospective employees an opportunity to make quick connections with current employees by way of shared interests outside of work.

▼ Tell 'Em What They've Already Got.

A recent internal survey conducted by Hoechst Celanese uncovered an amazing retention reality. They found that employees who were made aware of the company's already established work/life programs were almost 40 percent more likely to remain with the company for the next three years than employees who were not aware of the programs. Any culture can implement this best practice to improve employee retention.

▼ Flex Fit.

In 1992, Peat Marwick, the global service-driven consultancy, was facing a serious problem. It was about to lose many of its best employees simply because the company was not flexible regarding the employees' desire for more balanced work/life integration. In response, Peat Marwick began a program that offered part-time work, flex time, and flex hours to its employees, especially professional women who wanted to cut back on work hours to spend more time with family. Now, part-timers who work 1,000 hours receive benefits, and full-timers can work at home. Through helping their employees get a life, Peat Marwick continues to be a recognized service leader.

▼ I Forgive You.

Legacy Health System in Portland, Oregon, has a program to help employees become first-time home buyers. They provide forgivable, small financial loans to employees who buy homes in neighborhoods that need revival near Emanuel Hospital. Imagine the long-term connections generated to Legacy Health System through helping employees purchase a home.

▼ The Eleven-of-Twenty-Four Plan.

One service-driven culture found a unique way to provide additional service at little additional cost. Marquardt and Roche, a marketing agency in Stamford, Connecticut, was bogged down with employees asking for an additional paid holiday. Instead of giving everyone another holiday, Marquardt and Roche created a flexible holiday plan. At the beginning of the year, the company distributes a list of twenty-four holidays, from which employees can choose as many as eleven. As employees pick their preferred holidays, management balances the need for coverage. The result is that the employees now have a flexible holiday plan and the office is open more days than it was before the Eleven-of-Twenty-Four plan. This allows everyone to get a life while simultaneously extending customer contact days.

Best Practice Six in Action: In the Loop

Aligned organizations recognize that the more great employees feel in the loop of company information, the more likely they are to remain long-term employees. Here are several progressive ways aligned organizations improve retention through keeping employees informed.

▼ Minutes Within Minutes.

In the lightning-fast world of finance, minutes count. Nowhere is this truer than within the financial services environment of Raymond James Financial (first introduced in Chapter 8). Within minutes of completing an executive meeting, the minutes of that meeting are summarized and electronically posted throughout the company's intranet for all employees to see. Regardless of the core culture, Raymond James's minutes-within-minutes approach is a magnificent way to keep employees in the loop.

▾ GSD Call.

Every Tuesday morning at eleven, Larry Mercer, the executive vice president of operations for the Home Depot, conducts his weekly "get stuff done" (GSD) conference call to his division presidents and regional vice presidents. After a brief overview of operations, he gives his teams two things to get done in their stores *today*! The managers and VPs then relay the two items mentioned in the GSD call to their store managers throughout the Home Depot network. The GSD calls connect real-time issues with real-time results, while keeping service-minded employees in the loop on key performance areas.

▾ Open Meetings.

At the headquarters of Rosenbluth International all meetings are posted with an open invitation for anyone to attend. Any employee from any department can attend any meeting. Rosenbluth understands that often employees outside a particular department are just as emotional, passionate, and interested in the topic at hand as those inside the department.

▾ "Urgents" Board.

Lucent Technologies, based in Murray Hill, New Jersey, takes a creative yet simple approach to keeping employees in the loop and connected. It has a special place for listing orders that are behind schedule. Called the "urgents board," it's intended for Lucent employees with a few free minutes to jump into an urgent project and help their teammates get back on schedule.

▾ Passport, Please.

Interim Services, a temporary services company in Fort Lauderdale, connects with new hires uniquely. To get into the loop and connected fast at this service-driven company, all new hires are given what looks like a large passport book with the instructions to track down, meet, and talk to every senior manager and have them all stamp the passport. After accumulating all the stamps, new hires are invited to a special seminar, where they meet all the executives at once, learn about company history and culture, and ask questions of the senior staff. Interim's passport strategy is a great illustration of how to quickly build in-the-loop connections between new hires and the corporate culture.

▼ **V-Mail.**

During the acquisition of another drug retailer, Rite-Aid's chairman, Martin Grass, used an outside voice-mail system to receive anonymous feedback on issues important to employees of the acquired company. The system worked extremely well, with Grass being able to keep newly acquired employees in the loop through quickly responding to key issues of real concern. Any core culture can learn from Rite-Aid how to retain great employees during mergers and acquisitions.

▼ **Two-Minute Summaries.**

Every Monday morning at the headquarters of Windam Hill Records in Palo Alto, California, the company conducts a one-hour meeting for all of its thirty employees. Everyone gives a two-minute summary of what he or she plans to accomplish in the upcoming week. Rather than filter such goals through managers or written reports, a strong connection emerges between employees when each is asked to share individual goals collectively.

▼ **Hall Ways.**

Innovation-driven Adobe Systems, in San Jose, takes a simple approach to keeping people in the loop while avoiding long meetings in stuffy rooms. Adobe insists that all employees walk around and conduct meetings *in the hallways*. Believing that the best way to keep the information flowing is to get people out of their offices and mingling, Adobe finds many advantages to hall

meetings. First, it keeps the number of participants small so decisions can be reached far more quickly. Second, it forces people
to get to the point because they tire of standing up in a hallway.
Third, it significantly decreases status barriers while considerably increasing the personal connections among all levels of employees.

▼ **tickedoff.com.**

Many progressive companies are creating intranet Websites
for disgruntled employees to vent. Allowing employees to get
their feelings and thoughts out increases employee connections
to the company and to other employees who realize that someone else feels the same way. Additionally, it gives management a
real-time pulse of underlying employee concerns. From innovation-driven cultures like Netscape and Silicon Graphics to such
service cultures as Sears and operational-excellence cultures like
Wal-Mart, many leading companies are allowing their valued
employees an opportunity to get ticked off without reprimand.

▼ **Listening Posts.**

Customer feedback is critical to any company but especially important to customer-driven cultures. To help keep its
best employees in the loop, Lands' End sponsors internal meetings between frontline phone sales representatives and behind-
the-scenes workers. To maintain exceptional service levels,
Lands' End keeps a strong focus on the customer while building
stronger connections among all employees.

Best Practice Seven in Action: Lighten Up

Aligned organizations recognize that great employees are far
more likely to stay on for the long run if they can lighten up and
have a little fun. Here are several examples.

▼ **Have Fun or Get Fired.**

The unofficial mission at innovation-driven Paradigm

Communication, a St. Petersburg, Florida, software developer, is to "have fun or get fired." Realizing that high stress and long hours leave a workforce primed for massive burnout, Paradigm's owner, Dan Furlong, also enforces a specific and well-thought-out dress code and attendance policy. Here they both are in their entirety: "Show up for work, and wear something."

▼ **No-Class E-Mail.**

It can be incredibly frustrating trying to weed through mounds of e-mail, attempting to figure out which ones are important and which ones are not. Tandem Computers came up with a lighthearted twist to its internal communication system. Tandem now has three levels of internal e-mail. "First class" e-mail is all-business, and it should be read. Second-class e-mail is for interesting ideas and suggestions, a good place to go for hot topics and concepts. "No-class" e-mail is for humor and classified ads, a great place to stop when you need a quick mental break. This e-mail classification structure allows everyone at Tandem to quickly sort what is important, what's good to know, and what's just plain fun.

▼ **Back to School.**

The 1997 annual meeting for financial analysts at innovation-driven Cognex was organized like any other such meeting for that company: a day in elementary school! After being picked up in a yellow school bus, the analysts were driven to a meeting facility decked out with blackboards, carrying their lunchboxes, and even having pop quizzes. Naturally, the annual report was made to look like coloring books. What else would you expect from a company that calls all its employees "Cognoids" and carefully trains staff to properly execute their official company salute (modeled after—who else—the Three Stooges: right hand brought sharply to the bridge of the nose)? With the strength to lighten up, Cognex consistently attracts and retains great employees from throughout the Northeast.

▼ Stump the CEO.

Many great organizations are finding fun ways to keep executives in contact with employees while simultaneously showing the lighter side of business. One such company, AGI, a cosmetics packaging company in Melrose Park, Illinois, awards prizes during monthly employee meetings to the person who asks the CEO the toughest question. By demonstrating willingness to be held accountable for the tough issues and to do so in a humorous way, such organizations with a core culture of operational excellence create strong connections that help with retention of great employees.

▼ Be Loose and Have Fun.

Aligned companies need not have fancy, page-long, eloquently developed mission statements to retain great employees. Often, the simpler the better. One example comes from Great Harvest Bread, a spirit-driven franchise natural bread retailer based in Dillon, Montana, whose mission is to "be loose and have fun." Given only minimal operational guidelines, the franchise agreement specifically reads "Anything not expressly forbidden by the language of this document *is* allowed!" No two stores look alike. Franchisees are allowed to tinker with pricing and recipes. There are no home office inspections. By living their spirit-driven mission, Great Harvest builds powerful retention connections with its diverse franchisees.

▼ Happiness Barometer Team.

Appearing here yet again, Rosenbluth International travel group is known for its innovative, proactive employee-relations strategies. Management understands that happy employees are more productive and more likely to stay than are sad employees. One technique to keep tabs on employee morale is the "happiness barometer team," a group of employees charged with conducting a benchmark attitude and enjoyment-needs survey every six months. With a team name like this, employees realize that Rosenbluth is serious about their happiness, so why leave?

▼ **Let 'Em Surf.**

With facilities located near the Pacific Ocean in Ventura, California, the management team at Patagonia extends employees a very special perk tailored to their unique location. Realizing that you never know when great waves will come in, management allows employees to go surfing whenever they wish. With the flexibility to hit the beach when the waves are high, employee morale remains buoyant throughout the entire Patagonia facility. Just imagine another organization attempting to lure a Patagonia employee away when the employee asks about their surfing policy!

Best Practice Eight in Action: Free at Last

Aligned organizations understand that great employees can only remain that way within a culture that allows maximum freedom. Strong, long-term employee connections are built into a core culture that encourages initiative and freedom from bureaucracy. Here are several interesting examples of how organizations promote employee freedom.

▼ **Abolitionists.**

The executive team at SOL, a highly successful cleaning company in Finland, so embraces the concept of free-at-last that they have abolished every conceivable standard corporate perk. Within SOL, there are no titles, no secretaries, no individual offices, no set working hours, no status, and no special perks. Employees are free from the constraints of traditional status and the political fights that inevitably arise within conventional organizational systems, and they are therefore free to take whatever initiative is necessary to perform their duties. Besides, who would want to leave a service-driven company whose logo is a yellow happy face?

▼ First Memo of the Month.

Great employees thrive within environments that allow maximum freedom and a minimum number of directives from above. PSS/World Medical takes a fresh—and radical—approach to allowing employees to be free at last. Every office is required to read the first memo of the month sent from any officer. All other memos sent out from that officer that month can be ignored and summarily disposed. Within a service-driven culture, emancipating the freedom of action of employees impels phenomenal growth—and comparable retention.

▼ Scavenger Hunt.

Freedom is more than just a word at Southwest Airlines; it is instilled in employees from day one. To drive home the company's absolute, unrelenting passion for allowing employees the freedom to do their jobs, new hires at the corporate office participate in a scavenger hunt during orientation. Each person is given a list of questions about the history of Southwest Airlines. They are then told to roam the hallways, searching for the answers among the hundreds of photographs that line the walls of their three-story Dallas headquarters. They are also instructed to stop any employee or enter any office without making an appointment (including Chairman Herb Kelleher's office) in search of the answers. The scavenger hunt brilliantly connects fun with the Southwest Airlines operational-excellence culture, as well as communicating the freedom all employees have to do their work.

▼ Seven Mistakes a Day.

Mistakes are expected, and even encouraged, at Empower Trainers and Consulting, an Overland Park, Kansas, computer training and applications company. Every employee is exhorted to post his or her daily mistakes, preferably at least seven of them, on the office walls. Why seven? Founder and CEO Michael May believes that "if you're not making seven mistakes a day, you're just not trying hard enough."[1] Considered part of the corporate learning curve, mistakes are openly communicated within this service-driven culture to reinforce the freedom that employees have to experiment, test, and create new solutions for all customers. Creating an environment with the freedom to fail proactively promotes employee retention.

▼ Rolling Along.

At SEI Investments of Oaks Park, Pennsylvania, all office furniture is on wheels. Employees are therefore free to create their own workspace anywhere, and alongside anyone, to get the job done. Such freedom does create one interesting problem: How can you find a colleague when they do not have a fixed office? Since employees move their offices so often, SEI has created an electronic software map that helps employees within this innovation-driven investment company determine where their colleagues happen to be working that day.

▼ It's the Java Man.

Scott McNealy, CEO of Sun Microsystems in Palo Alto, California, learned a valuable lesson on employee freedom that has become part of the legacy of its innovation-driven culture. A few years ago, one of his top software engineers, Patrick Naughton, told McNealy he thought it impossible to be creative at Sun Microsystems and asked to be allowed to work on his own projects. Although Naughton was considered something of a critic and troublemaker, McNealy asked him to devise a plan to make it easier to be more innovative at the company. While working on the plan, the engineer began to design software that ultimately became the Internet standard and Sun's most successful product ever, Java. Connecting to someone's need for freedom, McNealy retained a great employee who eventually created a hugely successful, profitable product.

▼ Volunteer Day.

Demonstrating that great employees are trusted is a powerful retention device. AT&T recently took a huge step toward employee freedom. The company now gives all of the more than 100,000 employees an annual paid day off for volunteer work. Although not revolutionary in and of itself, this is the largest and most public corporate commitment toward community service in recent years. What sets this volunteer day apart, however, is the minimalist approach taken by AT&T management. Rather than requiring specific paperwork or reports on their work, employees need only clear their volunteer day with their supervisors—no other proof necessary. Simply and powerfully, AT&T demonstrates trust that its top employees do what they say—a powerful connection in building long-term employee retention.

NOTE

1. Nancy Austin, "The Culture Evolution," *Inc. 500 1997 Issue* (October 1997), pp. 72–80.

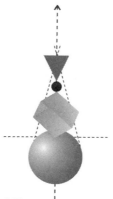

CHAPTER 12

ALIGNING RETENTION TO CORE CULTURE

This offers action ideas to help you begin aligning your retention practices to your core culture. As in Chapter 9, which offered ideas on staffing, here you might want to read first the section that applies to your core culture.

As you review the action ideas for your culture, consider the following:

▼ How can you implement the action item to improve your ability to keep great employees?
▼ How does the action item complement existing retention practices?
▼ What additional resources are needed to implement the action idea?

To create additional ideas for aligning retention to core culture, review the action ideas presented for the three other cultures. Remember that the same action idea may work for different cultures because although the gist of the action is the same in all four areas, the focus of the action is different for each core culture.

CUSTOMER SERVICE CULTURE

Here are seventeen ideas to begin aligning your retention practices to your service culture.

▼ Ask employees to list the top five roadblocks to creating customer solutions. Take immediate steps to minimize or eliminate each roadblock.

▼ Assess the degree to which all employees are able to reach out and touch the customer. Create cross-functional teams to generate new ways to connect with customers.

▼ Survey your superlative service employees for their top five examples of when a customer was wrong and how they responded. Summarize and circulate their responses to remind staff that even if the customer is wrong, the customer is always the customer.

▼ Celebrate and reward employees who take ownership of customers' problems without passing the buck.

▼ Assess how your management's internal feedback mechanisms connect to the real-time reaction needs of staff.

▼ Ask employees to rank the top three aspects of their service-focused job that most connect and engage their souls, and the three that most disconnect their souls. Build action plans to accentuate the connections and eliminate the disconnections.

▼ Rate on a scale of 1 to 10 how every monetary and nonmonetary recognition program drives your core culture to create customer solutions. Redesign those pay and rewards systems that do not clearly reinforce the core culture.

▼ Rate all training activities on how well they clearly reinforce your customer-solution processes. Redesign those that do not align.

▼ Align compensation and reward programs to encourage service-specific learning.

▼ Create opportunities for employees to experience the service-delivery methods of competitors. Encourage employees to share lessons learned at staff meetings, to include how competitors connect with them, how competitors communicate their expectations of customers, whether the competitor puts the customer first, and whether the competitor empowers employees. Integrate lessons learned into current and future customer-service training initiatives.

▼ Initiate a biannual "community service day." Encourage employees to volunteer one day of work each year to help teach a community group how to create solutions for its customers.

▼ Begin a one-page weekly internal newsletter, or its e-mail equivalent, on hot customer issues so as to keep staff in the loop. Include customer praises, problems, missed opportunities, and challenges to improve.

▼ Conduct information-sharing meetings between direct-customer-contact and behind-the-scene employees. Allow time to brainstorm solutions to improve delivery of customer solutions.

▼ Begin a quarterly contest on the funniest customer complaint, the weirdest customer expectation, and the silliest customer reaction. Offer employees lighthearted rewards for their willingness to create positive customer solutions even in unusual situations.

▼ Separate your e-mail into two major categories: service stuff (important customer issues) and other stuff (policy updates, general announcements, items of fun and interest). Encourage staff to read the service stuff first and save the other stuff for when they need a quick mental break or an update.

▼ Begin a "service mistake of the month" program. Encourage employees to recount service mistakes they made and share with all how to avoid the same mistake in the future. Reward the "winner" with $100 in cash.

▼ Organize a customer-call team to contact your top twenty customers. Ask each customer what three things they wish your frontline employees were given the freedom to do. Integrate their answers into your customer-service culture.

INNOVATION CULTURE

Here are fourteen ideas for increasing retention within your innovation-focused culture.

▼ Rank how well your internal communication programs reinforce key employee connections (need for speed, cannibalization, thrill of the adventure, etc.).

▼ Initiate a "serious fun" project rating system. Periodically ask employees to rate their level of fun on the company's serious projects.

▼ Create a cannibal committee. Direct the committee to meet each month and unleash its members' creative-destruction skills on a designated product, process, or company program. Recognize individual members who display a gift for cannibalism.

▼ Ask employees to list the top five roadblocks to creating the future. Take immediate steps to minimize or eliminate each roadblock.

▼ Survey employees for the five most time-consuming company practices. Redesign each practice around the need for speed.

▼ Ask employees to rank the top three aspects of their innovation-driven job that most connect and engage their souls, and the three that most disconnect and drain their souls. Build action plans to accentuate the connections and the positive; eliminate the disconnections and the negative.

▼ Rate on a scale from 1 to 10 how every monetary and nonmonetary recognition program drives your core culture to create the future. Redesign those rewards that do not clearly reinforce the core culture.

▼ Rate all training activities on how well they clearly reinforce your innovation-driven culture. Redesign those that do not align.

▼ Direct employees to plan an offsite outdoor adventure. Include fast, fun, and creative activities open to both employees and their significant others.

▼ Align compensation and reward programs to encourage innovation-specific learning.

▼ Initiate a biannual "community innovation day." Encourage employees to volunteer one day of work to help teach a community group how to create the future for its organization.

▼ Begin a "three F analysis." Before initiating any new project, have team members rate on a scale of 1 to 10 each of the project's potential three Fs: is it fast, focused, and fun? Any total rating below 25 must be redesigned.

▼ Rotate among your staff the two-week position of "innovation information initiator." Instruct the initiator to produce a biweekly one-page summary of hot industry trends, competitor initiatives, and how each has an impact on the company's business.

▼ Develop an annual goal of cannibalizing a minimum of 30 percent of your existing products. Conduct formal funerals for each cannibalized product—complete with toy airplane flyovers, flags at half-mast, and regal burials.

OPERATIONAL EXCELLENCE CULTURE

Use the following thirteen ideas to increase the retention of top talent within your operational excellence culture.

▼ Begin an "F-Troop contest." Based upon the idea of the television comedy's inept cavalry troop, pick your least efficient process and challenge your team to make fast quality improvements. Tell the team that when they reach the goals, you personally will call each member's spouse (mother, father, friend, roommate, or whomever they wish) and brag about how great you are until it hurts!

▼ Begin a "who's who of process improvement" directory for your company. Designate the champions of each process improvement by name and location. Highlight the big payoffs and efficiencies for each process.

▼ Commit to an annual "waste-away day." Reward the individual or team with the most original idea for eliminating waste by granting a day away from work.

▼ Ask employees to rank the top three aspects of their process-focused job that most connect and engage their souls. Also ask for the three aspects that most disconnect and drain their souls. Build action plans to accentuate the positive and eliminate the negative.

▼ Begin a weekly "process pipeline" voice-mail update focusing on the week's most notable process improvements. Recognize improvements in standards, error rates, and waste elimination.

▼ Rate on a scale from 1 to 10 how every monetary and nonmonetary recognition program drives your core culture to create the process. Redesign those rewards that do not clearly reinforce the core culture.

▼ Conduct a quarterly "Herbie heroes" party, celebrating those employees who overcame another process delay.

▼ Ask for volunteers to form a "balancing act" committee. Assign them to generate efficient, easy-to-implement guidelines and an action plan to better integrate work and balance in personal life.

▼ Rate all employee training activities on how well they clearly and directly reinforce your process-driven culture. Redesign those that do not align.

▼ Minimize wasted time by selecting one action a month that no longer requires your sign-off or approval.

▼ Align compensation and reward programs to encourage process-specific learning.

▼ Initiate a biannual "community operational excellence day." Encourage employees to volunteer one day of work to help teach a community group how to create processes of operational excellence within its organization.

▼ Designate a five-person team as the "line-up committee," charged with ensuring that all measures of employee success align with the company's overall measures of success.

SPIRIT CULTURE

Use the fourteen ideas to better align your retention practices to your spirit-driven culture.

▼ Distribute to all frontline employees a quarterly survey that asks only one question: What can management do to better serve you? Organize a cross-functional team to create and circulate an action plan that addresses the top issues.

▼ Form a "spirit committee," comprising volunteers who meet regularly to brainstorm ways to keep the spirit alive in your company. Give them a small budget and a quick target date to do something, and celebrate successes.

▼ Ask employees to list the top five roadblocks to creating an environment of spirit. Take immediate steps to minimize or eliminate each roadblock.

▼ Begin your next staff meeting with the question, "Why do you work here?" Integrate spirit-oriented responses into the discussion agenda, thereby demonstrating a strong connection between the employee's needs and the company's.

▼ Initiate a "special spirit FUN-raiser" campaign. Allow employees to organize and conduct a fund-raising campaign for a nonprofit organization. Let employees vote on organization to designate as the recipient.

▼ Ask employees to rank the top three aspects of their service-focused jobs that most connect and engage their souls. Also ask for the three aspects that most disconnect and drain their souls. Build action plans to accentuate the positive and eliminate the negative.

▼ Assess your entire work environment. Is servant leadership obvious? Are people really inspired to work for a greater good? Do you build people first, or things? Is your environment both competitive and humane?

▼ Rate on a scale from 1 to 10 how every pay and recognition program drives your core culture to create the environment. Redesign those rewards that do not clearly reinforce the core culture.

▼ Sponsor a "show-off day," when family and friends are invited into the workplace for employees to show off the special spirit at work.

▼ Rate all employee training activities on how well they clearly and directly reinforce your spirit-driven culture. Redesign those that do not align.

▼ Align compensation and reward programs to service-specific learning.

▼ Sponsor "gospel truth days" (that is, good-news days), where only good business news can be shared. It may be very quiet at first, but the momentum picks up considerably once the special spirit of good news starts permeating the workplace.

▼ Initiate a biannual community spirit day. Encourage employees to volunteer one day of work to help teach a community group how to create a spirit-driven environment in its organization. Begin a company scrapbook on the success stories of the community groups.

▼ Assign senior executives to one drudge job per week: making coffee, cleaning break room dishes, making photocopies, distributing mail, etc. Strive to have all executives demonstrate the spirit of servant leadership while participating in their drudge work.

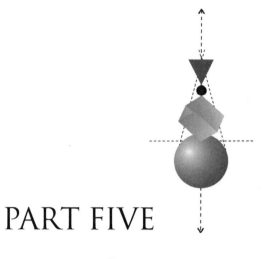

PART FIVE

GETTING
STARTED

CHAPTER 13: LEADING THE CHARGE

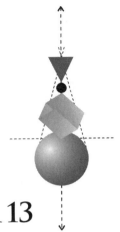

CHAPTER 13

LEADING THE CHARGE

You have read this book, you believe in the ability of culture to break the cycle of disconnection, and you understand the competitive advantage gained by aligning your staffing and retention strategies to your company's core culture.

Many business books inspire people to take action in their own organization. Frequently, though, no action follows—because people do not know how to get started. They do not have a plan to help them apply what's in the book to their company.

In this chapter, we describe a six-step process to help your company become more like the aligned companies described in this book. By following this process, you too can find and keep great employees.

STEP ONE: CLEARLY EMBRACE ONE CORE CULTURE

Before you can align your staffing and retention practices to your organization's culture, you must first know your culture.

To determine your company's culture, look at which actions are rewarded, which are punished, which decisions are supported and implemented, and which are ignored or challenged. Focus on the day-to-day organizational decisions and actions to better understand the core purpose underlying them. Talk to employees at all levels in the organization to understand their perceptions of the culture and to identify the most prevalent connections felt by your employees to the company and their jobs.

This is the most important and difficult step in the alignment process. It's the most important because it lays the foundation for alignment and impels the changes you make in your staffing and retention practices. It's the most difficult because it requires honesty. You must identify what your real culture actually is, not what sounds good or what you want it to be.

Culture is not typically found in the lofty statements of your company's mission or vision statement. It is also not based on catchy slogans or phrases ("Employees are our most important asset"; "Quality is number one"; and so on). Those slogans bear truth only if the organization supports actions and decisions that are consistent with the words. If you are unsure of your organization's core culture, refer to the four culture chapters (3 through 6) and review the cultural connection information there. Think about which cultural connections apply most to your organization.

After you identify your core culture, you may decide that another one best fits your organization's long-term, strategic objectives. If that's the case, then you should not attempt to align your staffing and retention strategies to your company's current core culture at this time. However, assuming you are able to identify your company's core culture, you then need to prioritize your actions for moving toward alignment.

STEP TWO: PRIORITIZE YOUR ALIGNMENT EFFORTS

If your organization is like most, you have strengths and weaknesses when it comes to your ability to find and keep great employees. Ideally, you want to take those things you do well to another level, and you want to improve your weaknesses. To do this, you must focus your efforts. No company has unlimited resources; therefore, no company can do everything when it comes to alignment.

To most effectively align your staffing and retention practices to your organization's core culture, you must prioritize your efforts. To do that, briefly describe two or three examples of the eight staffing best practices and the eight retention best practices in your organization (the WOW factor, applicant as customer, engage the soul, what gets rewarded gets done, etc.). For staffing, you may have several strong examples of two or three best practices and no examples for one or two of them. The same is true for the retention best practices.

Based on your examples, identify staffing and retention best practices that you currently do well, along with those that you need to improve. Generate some initial ideas on how you can better leverage those best practices that you currently do well. Identify ways you can implement or improve those staffing and retention best practices that you do not perform well.

STEP THREE: OBTAIN EMPLOYEE FEEDBACK
ON ALIGNMENT

Involve employees from all levels and locations in your organization's move toward alignment. A cross-section of employees needs to be involved in this process, for two reasons. First, the company benefits from different people's expertise and perspectives on specific alignment priorities. The more perspectives that are represented and the more knowledge that is included in this process, the better and more effective your company's alignment efforts are. A second reason for involving employees early in the alignment process is to ensure maximum buy-in on changes that are to occur in staffing and retention programs and processes.

You need to obtain employee feedback in a number of staffing and retention priority areas:

▼ Which staffing and retention materials and processes are aligned with the company's core culture? Which ones are not?

▼ What is the best way to align those staffing and retention materials and processes that are not aligned to the company's core culture?

▼ Who needs to be involved at different points in the alignment process?

▼ How are the newly aligned activities and materials to be monitored and evaluated?

▼ Which aspects of the organization make alignment easy, and what organizational barriers exist to alignment?

You may not use everyone's suggestions and feedback, but different employee perspectives need to be heard for alignment outcomes to be most effective. If you do not use a particular suggestion or recommendation, explain to employees why that idea cannot be used at this time.

STEP FOUR: CREATE ALIGNMENT INITIATIVES

Using the employee feedback obtained in step three, create new staffing and retention alignment initiatives and revise current staffing and retention programs. Employees need to be involved in this process as well. Although the focus is on staffing and retention programs, human resources should not be solely responsible for creating or revising these programs. The entire company benefits from these programs, so representatives from all areas should be involved in creating various alignment initiatives. To further ensure that the alignment process produces the most effective results, employees involved in this process need to work together and set time frames for implementing new staffing and retention programs and revising current ones.

STEP FIVE: IMPLEMENT ALIGNMENT INITIATIVES

If steps one through four have been effectively executed, implementation of aligned staffing and retention programs should be automatic. We recommend that you stagger implementation of various alignment initiatives over time. We also recommend that new initiatives be pilot-tested and refined. Staggered scheduling and pilot testing ensures that new processes and programs can be monitored and evaluated most effectively.

STEP SIX: MONITOR AND EVALUATE ALIGNMENT INITIATIVES

Effective alignment is not a single event but rather an ongoing process. New staffing and retention programs that are implemented need to be monitored and evaluated periodically. Then program changes have to be made based on that evaluation. Prior to implementing new programs, evaluation measures must be defined and developed. After the initial evaluation, a decision is made about the feasibility of the program being implemented companywide. Assuming a new staffing or retention program is implemented, the program continues to be monitored for effectiveness.

Any significant changes within the organization (such as change in executive leadership, merger, or significant acquisition) may require reanalysis of your core culture. Based on that reanalysis, staffing and retention programs might need to be changed because the company's core purpose has changed. In this case, the alignment process starts all over again.

MOVING FORWARD

After reading this book (and in particular, this chapter), you may feel that you do not have the time or resources to align your organization's staffing and retention functions to your core culture. Yet you must move forward. You face, on a daily basis, the great challenge of finding and keeping great employees. The challenge is not going away; in fact, it is likely to become even greater in the future.

The longer you do nothing, the worse the cycle of disconnection within your organization becomes. Hiring simply for job fit is not sufficient to meet the challenge. In the short term, throwing money at applicants and employees may help you hire and retain; however, there is no long-term payoff to the organization in such a practice. There is only one option: alignment.

To gain long-term competitive advantage, companies must provide deep, long-lasting, and purpose-driven focus so that applicants and employees can best connect to their company and their jobs. You now have the information and tools to move forward and create those powerful connections so that you can find and keep great employees.

RECOMMENDED
READINGS

Aiming Higher: 25 Stories of How Companies Prosper by Combining Sound Management and Social Vision, by David Bollier (New York: AMACOM, 1996). Presents the stories of twenty-five honorees of the Business Enterprise Trust, an organization that honors companies and individuals who have demonstrated bold, creative leadership by combining sound business management with social conscience. Addresses the complicated, difficult challenges met and overcome by businesspeople who hold themselves and their companies accountable for social change.

Ben & Jerry's Double Dip: Lead With Your Values and Make Money, Too, by Ben Cohen and Jerry Greenfield (New York: Simon & Schuster, 1997). Describes the unique and highly successful management philosophy of Ben & Jerry's Homemade. Explains their "value-led business" approach; discusses why this approach is the best model for business today; and tells how anyone who owns, works for, invests in, or shops with a company can help make it a socially responsible business.

The Connected Corporation: How Leading Companies Win Through Customer-Supplier Alliances by Jordan D. Lewis (New York: Free Press, 1995). Presents real-world experience and worldwide research in best-practice firms such as Chrysler, Du

Pont, Motorola, and Marks and Spencer. Describes how creating and sustaining customer-supplier alliances enables companies to lower costs, raise quality, decrease cycle times, and increase value for customers without adding expense.

Control Your Own Destiny or Someone Else Will, by Noel Tichy and Stratford Sherman (New York: Currency Doubleday, 1993). Offers an in-depth look at the leadership approach of CEO Jack Welch through GE's corporate transformation process. Includes a valuable three-step "handbook for revolutionaries" to guide your transformational journey.

Creating an "Open Book" Organization:... Where Employees Think & Act Like Business Partners, by Thomas J. McCoy (New York: AMACOM, 1996). Provides a practical, step-by-step approach to developing an effective partnership between management and staff. Outlines ways to educate employees about the business and their specific roles in the business, to understand and appreciate the company's best interests, and to encourage employees in this management approach through incentive plans.

The Culture of Success: Building a Sustained Competitive Advantage by Living Your Corporate Beliefs, by John Zimmerman with Ben Tregoe (New York: McGraw-Hill, 1997). Describes how a company's basic beliefs can affect long-term corporate growth, excellence, and even survival. Provides real-world examples from in-depth research conducted at such companies as Harley-Davidson, the American Automobile Association, J. M. Smucker, and Barnett Banks. Provides the process, tools, and inspiration to examine and energize corporate beliefs so that they guide the decisions and behavior of every employee to produce sustained success.

Customer Centered Growth: Five Proven Strategies for Building Competitive Advantage, by Richard Whiteley and Diane Hessan (Portland, Ore.: Perseus Press, 1996). Describes how companies have improved profits and grown—despite trends of cost cutting, downsizing, and divesting—by keeping the customer as the primary focus. Provides tools for self-assessment and strategic planning.

The Customer Comes Second: And Other Secrets of Exceptional Service, by Hal Rosenbluth and Diane McFerrin Peters (New York: William Morrow, 1992). The story of how Rosenbluth International became a multibillion-dollar global travel agency by putting its people first. Easy to read, with dozens of examples of how Rosenbluth International drives its spirit-driven culture.

Delivering Knock Your Socks Off Service, by Kristin Anderson and Ron Zemke (New York: AMACOM, 1998). A classic in how to build a service-driven company. Loaded with tips and advice, and written in an enjoyable style.

The 8 Practices of Exceptional Companies: How Great Organizations Make the Most of Their Human Assets, by Jack Fitz-enz (New York: AMACOM, 1997). Documents the most enduring best practices in human asset management, based on four years of in-depth research at more than 1,000 companies. Describes specific examples of these best practices and how companies that excel in both profitability and employee retention handle change management, cost reduction, employee turnover, productivity, quality improvement, and the other challenges that all companies face.

Getting Employees to Fall in Love With Your Company, by Jim Harris (New York: AMACOM, 1996). An easy, quick read of more than 130 bite-sized best-people practices organized by five easy-to-remember principles. Three in-depth case studies illustrate how to apply the five-part model across diverse industries.

Innovation: Breakthrough Thinking at 3M, Du Pont, GE, Pfizer, and Rubbermaid, by Rosabeth Moss Kanter, Fred Wiersema, John J. Kao, and Tom Peters (New York: HarperBusiness, 1997). Examines how the five visionary companies in the title and others improved their operations through flattened hierarchies, open communication, and inventive thinking. Presents case studies written by executives at 3M, Du Pont, GE, Pfizer, and Rubbermaid that demonstrate the importance of innovation in each company's long-term success.

Lean Thinking: Banish Waste and Create Wealth in Your Organization, by James P. Womack and Daniel T. Jones (New York: Simon & Schuster, 1996). Describes what lean management is, how it works, and how it can help anyone create a more profitable organization through effective streamlining of strategies and techniques. Examines the successes at twenty-five U.S., Japanese, and German companies that have effectively implemented the "lean principles" of value, value stream, flow, pull, and perfection.

The Loyalty Effect: The Hidden Force Behind Growth, Profits, and Lasting Value, by Frederick F. Reichheld (Boston: Harvard Business School Press, 1996). Demonstrates the power of loyalty-based management as a highly profitable alternative to the economics of perpetual churn. Describes the principles that connect value creation, loyalty, growth, and profits; and shows how companies such as State Farm, Toyota/Lexus, MBNA Corporation, John Deere, and the Leo Burnett advertising agency have used these principles to build unparalleled franchises and loyal customers, loyal employees, and loyal owners.

Managing by Values, by Ken Blanchard and Michael O'Connor (San Francisco: Berrett-Koehler, 1996). Describes how companies can manage with common vision by creating a plan that clarifies, communicates, and aligns the organization's practices in all areas. Goes beyond the standard measures of success in the corporate world—size and volume—to describe a way of assessing a company's success based on the quality of service available to its customers and the quality of life afforded its employees.

Nuts! Southwest Airlines' Crazy Recipe for Business and Personal Success, by Kevin Freiberg and Jackie Freiberg (Austin, Texas: Bard Press, 1996). Provides an insider's perspective on the management philosophy and practices of Southwest Airlines. Describes the influence of these management practices on individual employees and organizational performance through hundreds of examples from within the company.

Organizing Genius: The Secrets of Creative Collaboration, by Warren Bennis and Patricia Ward Biederman (Portland, Ore.: Perseus Press, 1998). Describes how successful companies are gaining "collaborative advantage" through assembling powerful teams. Presents six case studies, from organizations such as Xerox and Disney, that examine the characteristics of successful collaboration and how talent can be pooled and managed for greater results.

The Power of Alignment, by George Labovitz and Victor Rosansky (New York: Wiley, 1997). Describes how linking the five key elements of an organization—people, process, customers, business strategies, and leadership—results in sustained growth and profit, loyal customers, and a high-performing workforce. Provides real-world examples of world-class companies achieving extraordinary business results through alignment.

Reclaiming Higher Ground: Creating Organizations That Inspire the Soul, by Lance H. K. Secretan (New York: McGraw-Hill, 1997). Presents an innovative plan for organizational change that encourages putting heart and soul into the workplace as a way of building business values, productivity, and profit. Offers solutions and personal checklists for readers to assess their progress in reclaiming the higher ground by way of a foundation built on trust and integrity.

The Soul of the Firm, by C. William Pollard (New York: HarperBusiness and Zondervan, divisions of HarperCollins, 1996). Describes the amazing story of ServiceMaster, the leading service company in the world, and how they achieved twenty-five consecutive years of growth in revenues and profits. Provides a revolutionary plan for new leadership that considers the critical link between people and profits in a company's measure of success.

Staffing the New Workplace: Selecting and Promoting for Quality Improvement, by Ronald B. Morgan and Jack E. Smith (Milwaukee: ASQC Press, 1996). Describes how to design and implement a staffing effort that supports a company's quality initiative. Presents specific techniques for recruiting, assessing, selecting, and promoting employees for a workplace focused on delivering quality goods and services.

Winning Through Innovation: A Practical Guide to Leading Organizational Change and Renewal, by Michael L. Tushman and Charles A. O'Reilly III (Boston: Harvard Business School Press, 1997). Describes how short-term success can increase the likelihood of long-term failure, using corporate examples from Disney, 3M, Compaq, and FedEx. Presents a framework for companies on how to overcome the "success syndrome" and develop action plans to ensure a constant supply of "innovation streams," to continuously develop new and better products and services.

INDEX